MIDDLE ENGLISH SURNAMES IN WEST YORKSHIRE

Wendi A. Dunlap

Three Beacons Press
Seattle, WA

Copyright © 2013 Wendi A. Dunlap

All rights reserved.

Cover photos by the author.

Three Beacons Press
2921 17th Ave S
Seattle, WA 98144

ISBN-13: 978-0615905273
ISBN-10: 0615905277

To the many authors, writers,
researchers and history-geek friends
who kindled and nurtured my interest in the study
of medieval names.

Table of Contents

Introduction	5
English Surnames	11
A brief introduction to the Wakefield Rolls	29
Classification of the Wakefield Names	33
Names in their time	47
Conclusions	57
The names	61
Appendix I: Bibliography	239
Appendix II: Maps	247

One:

Introduction

By the fifteenth century in England, the process of adopting hereditary surnames was nearly completed. This process began near the time of the Norman Conquest with names adopted by the upper classes and then moved on to the populace in the southern part of England, first with descriptive bynames, then with true hereditary surnames. Gradually over the next few centuries, surnames spread both geographically northward and socially outward through the merchant classes and peasantry. Hereditary surnames developed somewhat later in Yorkshire than they did further south.[1]

The Wakefield Court Rolls are records of manorial court proceedings from the sprawling Wakefield Manor in the West Riding of Yorkshire. The earliest Roll extant is from 1274, and the records continue, with some breaks,

---

[1] Reaney, P.H. *A Dictionary of English Surnames*. 3rd Edition p. li.

until the 1920s. As records of the activity on the Manor, the Rolls contain many surnames of Wakefield-area residents.

The Rolls from the period of 1274-1352 are especially interesting in that they contain a snapshot of Yorkshire names during the period in which surnames in that area were undergoing change, being more widely adopted, and although they were on the verge of becoming fixed and hereditary, they were still somewhat fluid. This fluidity means that the surnames of people mentioned in the rolls are able to provide us with a picture of the lives of these medieval Yorkshire people that later hereditary surnames cannot; a surname from this period often describes its bearer's occupation, home, relationship, or personality, not merely his (or her) name.

Through the work of the Yorkshire Archaeological Society since the late nineteenth century, quite a few volumes of the Wakefield Rolls have been translated and published. As such, they are an accessible and rich source of onomastic information. Though names from the Rolls have been used in several previous works,[2] I am not aware of any attempts to publish an analysis of large numbers of late medieval names specifically from this source.

There are some limitations to these sources. As they are English translations of a Latin original, there is some possibility of mistranslation. However, the earliest records,

---

[2] *Yorkshire West Riding (English Surnames Series I)* by George Redmonds is the most notable example.

from 1274-75, have been published both in Latin and in English, so I have been able to cross-check some of the translated content with the Latin text, though of course there is some risk of mistranscription in the Latin text as well. There is also some risk that the translators may have normalized or modernized some of the names to forms that are misleading; however, the translators generally seem not to have done this,[3] and in the case of the earliest Rolls this can be verified by checking the Latin text.

It can be difficult to evaluate how representative these records are of the population of the manor since the free and landless would not owe suit of court;[4] however, tenants were required to attend, and the type of cases that were brought up in court would have involved people of all classes. Indeed, we see cases involving knights and ladies as well as cases involving servants. In this sense, it seems fairly representative of the population of the manor at that time.

One further limitation to the data in the Rolls is that women are not listed nearly as often as men. Women's names make up only 10% of the total names mentioned in the thirteenth-century records examined here. In the mid-

---

[3] Surnames are not modernized or normalized by the translators, but given names usually are. However, this does not typically affect the surname data in this work.

[4] Goldberg, P.J.P. *Women, Work, and Life Cycle in a Medieval Economy: Women in York and Yorkshire c. 1300-1520* p. 29.

fourteenth century, the percentage of women mentioned does increase significantly to 24%. However, the period of 1350-52 is that of a "general air of dislocation" following the Black Death. Though the Rolls do not explicitly mention the plague, one may see its indirect effects throughout this period, including the January 1350 tourn at which it was noted that "the vill of Shelf is dead."[5] It seems likely that women are seen more frequently in court records of this period because they took roles in cases that might otherwise have been taken by men before the extreme mortality of the plague.

This study included 2,313 names: 1,148 names from the 1270s, and 1,165 names from the 1350s. The names do change during that period. In the earliest Rolls, the largest number of bynames are locative, many names are given as Latin translations of English descriptive terms, and many people do not have a byname. By the 1350s, in the immediate aftermath of the Black Death, bynames are nearly universal. The largest number of names are relationship names, names that were previously Latin are now in English, and there is some evidence that some names may be hereditary surnames.

---

[5] Habberjam, Moira, Mary O'Regan, and Brian Fraser, eds. *Court Rolls of the Manor of Wakefield: From October 1350 to September 1352* pp. xxii, xii; Jewell, Helen M., ed. *Court Rolls of the Manor of Wakefield: From September 1348 to September 1350* p. 225.

The surnames in the Rolls include names of the local, relationship, occupational, and nickname type, and each one of these types gives us insight into the Wakefield-area society.

The large number of local names, particularly in the earlier Rolls, imply an importance of place in a bearer's identity, and illustrate that some level of mobility existed in this society although most names refer to nearby West Riding places.

Relationship names, most common in the later Rolls, show us typically identifying relationships such as "son of/daughter of/wife of X (male)," but, surprisingly, they include a large number of matronymic bynames, in which the bearer is defined by his or her mother instead of father.

Occupational names, although less common than other types, are plentiful, and give a clear picture of the occupations carried out in the Wakefield area.

Nicknames, perhaps the most interesting and unusual name type, give us a particularly picturesque insight into the medieval personality, including names that are metaphorical and even uncomplimentary. The Wakefield names, then, illustrate a particularly interesting selection of naming practices during a rapidly changing time.

Two:

English Surnames

An overview

In 1000 CE, the typical English person bore a single name; by 1500, the hereditary surname was nearly universal. During the intervening years, surnames in England gradually developed from informal nicknames or bynames into fossilized hereditary family names, which may be categorized into four name classes: local names, names of occupation, names of relationship, and nicknames.[6]

Naming in pre-Conquest England followed a typical Germanic pattern. Each person had a single name. Often this name was chosen from a group of name elements that belonged to the family and were handed down from generation to generation. Examples include names such as *Theuderic* and *Theudebald*, with the repeating *Theud-* ("people, folk") element, or *Æthelred*, *Æthelstan*, and

---

[6] Reaney, *The Origin of English Surnames* p. 20.

Æthelfleda, with *Æthel-* "noble".⁷ Other names were shorter names, drawn from single Old English root words (*Budda*, *Lēof*) or from the longer compound names (*e.g. Wine*, from *Winefrid*).⁸

Of course, some people at this time had nicknames or bynames as well (an example P.H. Reaney mentions is *Ælfuuard æt Dentune*, in the late tenth century), but these were not hereditary.⁹ Reaney points out that at their core all surnames are essentially nicknames and were originally given according to no particular rule. People frequently had more than one such nickname, just as today many people have different nicknames in different contexts.¹⁰. Ælfuuard æt Dentune (Ælfward of Denton), might also have been called Ælfward the miller, Ælfward the redhead, or Ælfward the younger, depending on the context at various times.

Naming in Norman England, understandably, developed in parallel to the naming practices in France. During the eleventh century CE in both France and

---

⁷ Gies, Frances and Joseph Gies. Marriage and Family in the Middle Ages p. 51; Reaney, *Origin* p. 99; Weekley, Ernest. *Surnames* pp. 40, 43.

⁸ Hjertstedt, Ingrid. *Middle English Nicknames in the Lay Subsidy Rolls for Warwickshire* p. 14.

⁹ Reaney, *Origin* p. 296.

¹⁰ *Ibid.* pp. 19-20.

England, even members of the nobility typically had simple Germanic names,[11] sometimes followed by a local descriptive byname such as *de Seignelay,* "of the manor of Seignelay." This was not yet hereditary, or even specifically familial. Knights of the Seignelay manor, for example, might also bear the byname *de Seignelay* until they gained their own estates and with them their own descriptive bynames.[12]

Under Norman influence, the Old English naming system slowly died out; however, Old English names existed alongside the newer names well into the period of surname formation. These names are the source of quite a few Modern English surnames.[13]

As with many customs, the use of hereditary surnames started at the higher strata of society and gradually percolated down to the lower classes. Additionally, the adoption of surnames in the northern part of England was about 50 years behind the south.[14]

---

[11] The naming practices of the Gaelic and Brythonic minorities in Britain and France did differ somewhat, notably in a stronger reliance on names of relationship. Gaelic and Brythonic names appear to be nearly nonexistent during this period in West Yorkshire, so I will not discuss them.

[12] Gies and Gies p. 127.

[13] Hjertstedt p. 15.

[14] Reaney, *Origin* pp. 312-314.

Surnames of the landed classes began to become hereditary during the eleventh and twelfth centuries, and for the rest of society shortly afterward. However, they were clearly still not universally stable in the late thirteenth and early fourteenth centuries in Yorkshire, when the Wakefield Court Rolls in the West Riding include several examples of surnameless villeins (*e.g.* Pouwe), or father/son pairs with differing surnames (*e.g.* Richard del Rodes and Serlo de Ossete, or Gerbot de Alvirthorpe and his sons John Schirloc, Adam Gerbot, Walter son of Gerbot, and Richard Gerbot).

In nearby Lancashire in the late fourteenth century, a substantial number of people in the records were still listed in records only by first names and relationship terms such as *filius de*, -*son*, -*doghter*, and –*wyf*, which are generally authentically descriptive.[15] This type of name is also the most common in the Wakefield Rolls during the 1350s.

People throughout the fourteenth century were still frequently referenced by differing bynames depending on the context, or even by multiple descriptive bynames, any one of which may have later developed into the hereditary surname. An example given by Reaney is Richard Poche of Preston called le Belleyetere, whose descendants may have eventually been known as Pouches, Prestons, or Billiters.[16]

---

[15] Hey, David. *Family Names and Family History* p 66.

[16] Reaney, *Origin* p. 20.

Bynames were not as solid a part of one's identity as they are today; a man marrying a widowed heiress might adopt the name of the woman's previous husband.[17] According to Reaney, such variation may be found as late as the seventeenth century, if sporadically, but by the end of the fifteenth century, hereditary surnames were generally in place.[18]

During the twelfth century and later, there was a sharp decrease in the number of given names that were commonly used, and this, perhaps, was one of the causes for the increase in surname use, in order to distinguish people who could no longer be distinguished by a semi-unique family given name. David Hey cites a 1379 poll tax return in which 715 men have only 20 different given names among them, and thirty-three percent of them are named *John*.[19] A graphic example of this limited range of given names may be seen in the Wakefield Rolls, where this list of 12 jurors' names in 1315 is typical:

> Jurors. Alexander of the Frith, John Flemyng of Dalton, John of Querneby, Thomas of Tothill, John Flemyng of Clifton, Master Thomas of Dalton, John son of John of Lokwode, Roger of the Haghe, John

---

[17] Gies and Gies pp. 166-167.

[18] Reaney, *Origin* pp. 305, 315-316.

[19] Hey p. 55.

Clerk of Hertesheved, Henry of Coldelay, John of Birstall, & William Squier [. . .].[20]

Another jury only a few days later includes four Adams, three Richards, two Henrys, two Johns, and one Hugh.[21] In this sea of Johns, Adams, and Richards, it is easy to understand why bynames became necessary for recognition.

Local Surnames

The most common type of surnames found in most Middle English-period records are local surnames. These were generally names that described where someone originated, lived or worked, and can be divided into two types: locative, and topographical.

Locative names refer to towns, villages, estates, or even regions and countries: Adam de Salesbury came from Salisbury, and Adam de Bidyk was from Biddick.[22] In some

---

[20] Lister, John, ed. and trans. *Court Rolls of The Manor of Wakefield, Volume IV, 1315-1317* p. 17

[21] *Ibid.* p. 20.

[22] Reaney, Origin p. 47. In names such as *Adam de Salesbury*, *de* is the Latin documentary form. The English vernacular used in speech or English language documents was probably simply "of." The Latin form is usually found in the Wakefield records, which were kept in Latin at this time.

cases, these surnames came from estates owned by the family, but in other cases the families were farmers or villeins, not necessarily the owners of any property that gave them their surname.[23] Reaney mentions that in many cases, such names represented a place of origin but not necessarily a current residence. They were "a convenient means of identifying a newcomer": for example, *de London* might describe a person newly arrived from London and *de Callis* one from Calais.[24]

Topographical names come not from place names but from landscape features, such as a green, a bridge, a river, or a hill. Adam *Ithelane* probably lived in the lane, Sarra *Bithebrok* probably lived by a brook, and Simon *atte Hegge* probably lived by a hedge.[25] Examples of this type of name in the Wakefield Rolls include Richard *Attounend*, Adam *Attewelle*, Henry *Bythebrok*, and John *Bythesyk* (from *syke* "a ditch or small stream"). French and Latin forms were sometimes used as well; *ad Barram*, *ad capud ville*, and *de Bosco* were the equivalent, respectively, of *atte Barre* "at the bar," *Attounend* "at town's end," and *del Wode* "of the wood." In some cases the French and Latin forms are merely documentary forms, probably not used in

---

[23] Hey p. 75.

[24] Reaney, *Origin* p. 36.

[25] *Ibid.* p. 48.

speech, but in other cases they have survived as the spoken form[26].

Generally, the most common preposition in this type of name was a descendant of Old English *æt*, seen in such forms as *atten*, *atter*, and *atte*.[27] In many cases, these prepositions did not survive the Middle English period, but in others, they have survived (*e.g.* Wood, Atwood; Water, Atwater).[28]

Names of Occupation

Surnames of occupation developed from terms describing a person's job or role in the community. Examples of such descriptions are common in the late thirteenth-century Rolls, including *Robert pistor de Bretton* "baker of Bretton," *Hugh le Carectarius* "carter," *William Sutor* "cobbler," *Amabel le Harper*, and *Robert le Melemaker*. At that time, most of these names appear to be purely descriptive and not yet hereditary, and other early Yorkshire records confirm that occupational surnames were commonly descriptive in this period.[29] Eventually records start to show occupational surnames followed by descriptions of a different trade, (e.g. *John Faber, carnifex,*

---

[26] *Ibid.* p. 49.

[27] *Ibid.*

[28] Reaney, *Dictionary* pp. 18-19.

[29] *Ibid.* p. 1.

in Suffolk, 1327) and this is often an indication that the surname may have become fixed and is no longer literal.[30] These indications are very scarce in the Rolls during the late thirteenth through mid-fourteenth century, thus reinforcing Reaney's suggestion that hereditary surnames in Yorkshire were late to develop.

Names of Relationship

Surnames of relationship most commonly originated from nicknames describing a person's familial relationships, but sometimes they also reflect a master/servant relationship. Patronymics, names describing one's paternity, were used by most Germanic cultures, and indeed, literal patronymics are still used in Iceland today. These were not hereditary and only gradually came to be used as real family names instead of descriptions.[31] In the early Wakefield Rolls, we frequently see most such names as descriptive. In 1274, John is listed as "son of Hanne," but Hanne is "son of Ketyl," and no other surname is given for the father and son.[32]

Documents of the period commonly listed patronymics in Latin form, such as *Agnes filia Johannis del*

---

[30] Reaney, *Origin* p. 304.

[31] *Ibid.* pp. 75-76.

[32] Baildon p. 80.

Barm, or *Johannem filium Marie*.³³ These documentary forms were probably not used in the spoken vernacular; English records, instead, begin to show names such as *Gamel Grimessune* and *Ralf Maldessone*,³⁴ and the 1350-52 Rolls include many of this *–son* type.

Names of the *fitz-* type, such as the name translated as *Sir William fitzThomas* in the Wakefield Rolls, are Anglo-Norman in origin and reflect a corruption of Anglo-Norman *fis*, from Old French *fils*, which in turn reflected Latin *filius*.³⁵ In the case of Sir William, however, the court rolls give only the Latin form, *Dominus Willelmus filius Thomas*, and this is typical in Latin records of the time.³⁶ This being indistinguishable from other purely descriptive "son of" references in the records, it is difficult to pinpoint which names may have become hereditary *fitz-* names.³⁷

Names such as *Howeles* and *Paynes* are also frequently patronymics, with the surname using the genitive form: Howell's (son), Payne's (son).³⁸ Names of this type became more common throughout the fourteenth century, but they did not always represent a patronymic form. In some records husband and wife pairs can be found

---

[33] *Ibid.* pp. 29, 71.

[34] Reaney, *Origin* pp. 75-76.

[35] *Ibid.* p. 87, pp. 90-91.

[36] Baildon p. 64, p. 141.

[37] Reaney, *Origin* p. 91.

[38] *Ibid.*

such as *John Serle* and *Isabella Serles*, demonstrating that perhaps this genitive form could also have indicated a marital relationship.[39] In other cases the name might have reflected a servant or employee relationship (*Clerkes* and *Cokes* might be "servant of the clerk" and "servant of the cook"); however, in these cases this might also have been a patronym such as "son of the clerk" or "son of the cook."[40] Interestingly, although this genitive type of name is found elsewhere during this period, it is generally not seen in the Wakefield Rolls examined here.

Unmarked patronyms are surnames consisting solely of the given name of the father, such as the above-mentioned Adam and Richard Gerbot, both sons of Gerbot. These began to become common in documents from as early as the Conquest, and Reaney suggests that they may have been the most common spoken form; William, Dudda's son, would often have been *Willelmus filius Dudde* in documentary form but *William Dudde* in English speech. However, the form without *fili-* is seen in Latin texts as well.[41] It is common to find people listed with an unmarked patronym on one occasion, and a full patronym on another; in the Rolls, Adam Gerbot is sometimes called *Adam son of Gerbot*.

---

[39] *Ibid.* p. 92.

[40] *Ibid.* pp. 92-96.

[41] *Ibid.* pp. 97-98.

Like patronyms, matronyms were recorded in Latin documents. Examples in the Wakefield Rolls are many, including *Alanum filium Juliane* and *Johannem filium Marie*.⁴² As with patronyms, some of these were "unmarked" matronyms — no "filius/filia," but just the feminine surname (e.g. *Robert Gunnilt, William Mariot*), many of which have survived to this day in forms that obscure their source considerably.⁴³ Clear evidence that the byname is a parent's name may be found occasionally. An example is Robert, the son of Anot de Stanley, who is found in the thirteenth century Rolls as *Robertus filius Anot* as well as *Robertus Anot*.⁴⁴

These names do not necessarily mark illegitimacy. Other explanations for the matronymic form might include widowed mothers, posthumous birth, step-families, and families in which, as Reaney puts it, the mother was "notoriously, and in an emphatic sense, the better half."⁴⁵ Illegitimacy, however, is likely to be the reason for some names of this type, as well as for the surname *Bastard*, which still survives even though it is rare.⁴⁶

In addition to parental relationships, other family relationships were also noted in surnames of this period.

---

⁴² Baildon pp. 15, 19.

⁴³ Reaney, *Origin* p. 76

⁴⁴ Baildon pp. 92, 153, 156.

⁴⁵ Reaney, *Origin* p. 78

⁴⁶ *Ibid.* p. 79.

Ioseph frater Benjamin was Benjamin's brother, and *Gerardus nepos episcopi* was the bishop's nephew. English language examples are common, including *Childebroder*, *Prestesneve*, *Cosyn*, and the amusingly described *Fathevedstepson* "fathead stepson".[47] Other people bearing names more obscure to our eyes include John Odam, from Middle English *Odame* "brother-in-law, son-in-law"; and Radulfus Heam, whose Latin name *Radulfus avunculus* tells us that his English surname derives from the Middle English *eme* "uncle".[48] William Marjoriman, a bailiff in the Wakefield Manor, might have been married to a woman named Marjorie.[49]

Employee relationships were also the source of some bynames, as seen above with names such as *Cokes*. *Marjoriman*, too, may have been an employee name if William served a woman named Marjorie.[50]

Nicknames

Nicknames are perhaps the most colorful and interesting of early English surnames. Many of them are simple descriptions of the bearer's physical characteristics,

---

[47] *Ibid.* pp. 21, 80; Baildon p. 190.
[48] Lister p. 5; Reaney, *Origin* p. 81.
[49] Lister p. 129.
[50] Reaney, *Origin* pp. 192-193.

while others seem to be more esoteric. Reaney categorizes nicknames in surnames as follows:

- Physical and external peculiarities
- Mental and moral characteristics
- Nicknames from animals, birds, and fishes
- Names from oaths, street cries and phrase-names
- Names of indecent and obscene connotation[51]

There is one additional nickname category that overlaps with occupational bynames: the metonymic byname, in which an object is substituted for an occupation involving that object. For example, the Wakefield Rolls include Ralph *Hering*, who may have been a dealer in herrings, and Richard *Swerd*, who may have been a swordmaker.[52] However, without stronger evidence, it is usually difficult to be certain whether such names are truly metonyms or rather are true nicknames.

Physical characteristics mentioned in surnames include size, coloring, clothing, and other aspects of the bearer's appearance. Richard *Longschankes* or one of his ancestors probably had long legs, and Ellen *Schort* and Henry *Schorthose* were likely diminutive.[53] John *Schirlok* may have borne a different surname from his brothers,

---

[51] Reaney, *Origin* p. 232.

[52] Baildon, pp. 132, 84.

[53] Lister p. 8; Baildon pp. 117, 105.

Adam and Richard *Gerbot*, because he had shining blond locks of hair; *Schir-* derives from *scir*, which, in Old English, meant "bright, shining".[54] William *Grenehod* probably wore a green hood, and William *Wytbelt* may have been noted for his white belt.[55] Robert *the Leper*'s nickname is self-explanatory.[56]

Nicknames describing mental and moral characteristics were both complimentary and uncomplimentary, and examples of both are common.[57] William *Godyongman* may have been a good young man (or a good young servant, most likely) when he appeared in the Wakefield Rolls in 1315 for a land transaction, but perhaps his nickname was given ironically; in his next appearance in 1317, he was fined for "blood drawn from Agnes the Laundress's daughter".[58] Reaney gives examples of such insulting nicknames as *Thinnewyt* "thin of wit," *Mallorei* "unlucky," and *le Glutun*.[59] William *Yllewyly*'s byname refers to one who is of wicked will,[60] while Adam

---

[54] Baildon p. 290; Reaney, *Origin* p. 235.

[55] Baildon p. 250; Lister p. 99.

[56] *Ibid.* p. 155.

[57] Reaney, *Origin* p. 252.

[58] Lister pp. 16, 181.

[59] *Origin* p. 256-258.

[60] Baildon p. 92.

le Trikur may have been a deceiver,[61] and Richard *Sourmilk* may have sold sour milk.[62]

Complimentary nicknames, while not quite as entertaining, are found as well; Reaney cites *Swetemouth*, *Smart* and *Fayrwit* among others.[63] Examples in the Rolls include William *Godfelagh*, William *Hendebody* "comely and fair body," and Richard *Wyse*.[64]

The animal kingdom provided many nicknames. In some cases these may indicate that the bearer had some characteristic of a given animal, but in others they may reflect that the bearer worked with animals or lived or worked in a building with the sign of the animal. Examples include *Brok* "badger," *Fox*, and *Robug* (a male roe deer).[65] In Wakefield, there was a man bearing the surname *Wythehundes*,[66] and one wonders exactly why he was known for being "with the hounds." A few years later, Richard *Wytthehogges* was named similarly.[67]

Oath-names and expressions gave rise to some of the more picturesque Middle English surnames. Someone's favorite expression might be commemorated in a surname

---

[61] *Ibid.* p. 129.

[62] Habberjam p. 56.

[63] *Origin* pp. 252, 260.

[64] Habberjam pp. 17, 67; Baildon p. 153.

[65] Baildon pp. 147, 92, 119.

[66] *Ibid.* p. 293.

[67] Lister p. 44.

such as *Goodday*, *Drinkhale*, or *Allehaile*, and names such as *Godesgrace*, *Godsake*, and *Mouthergod* may perhaps tell us which oaths were frequently spoken by the person so named. The surname of one Hawisia *Crist a pes* records the saying "Christ have peace!" — and since her husband was known as Henry *Lytilprud* "little worth," one imagines easily why she might often have said it.[68] There are few certain examples of these types of names in the Wakefield names examined for this project, however one may be Robert *Pes*, who may have frequently used the interjection "Peace!"[69] Another may be John *Godale*, who may have said "Good ale!" as a sales pitch.[70]

As is obvious to anyone who has read Chaucer, the medieval English were not overly delicate in matters of language, and this is reflected in some of the names they bore. Adam Ballok's nickname did indeed probably refer to a testicle.[71] *Baisers* combined French *baise* "kiss" and English *ears* "arse"; *Brendhers* was a similar compound, the first part meaning "burn," and so this name would be suitable for the character of Nicholas in *The Miller's Tale*. The meaning of Rolland le Pettour's name, a French term, becomes clear when one sees that in another record he is listed as Roland *le Fartere*. Names such as this are mild,

---

[68] Reaney, *Origin* pp. 259, 276-279.

[69] Baildon p. 83.

[70] Habberjam p. 13.

[71] Baildon p. 326; Reaney, *Origin* p. 291.

however, in comparison to those of Richard *Scittebagge*, Simon *Sitbithecunte*, and Roger *Louestycke*.[72] Many names of this type have not survived or have been altered beyond all recognition to suit later sensibilities.

---

[72] To clarify: *sc* was pronounced "sh," and "v" was frequently spelled with a *u*.

Three:

A brief introduction to the Rolls

The names to be examined in this book are found in the Wakefield Manor Court Rolls, which are the records of the Manor of Wakefield, a large and populous manor in the historic West Riding of Yorkshire.

The town of Wakefield was "the traditional capital of the West Riding" according to A. H. Smith, who suggests that the town's importance as a meeting place for the southern part of the Riding dates to before the Conquest.[73] The name "Wakefield" may itself give some indication of the town's early role as a periodic gathering site; the name is thought to be derived from Old English

---

[73] Smith, A. H. *The Place-Names of the West Riding of Yorkshire, Part II: Osgoldcross and Agbrigg Wapentakes*, pp. 163-164.

wacu "watch, wake" and *feld* "open land," meaning "the open land where an annual wake or festival occurs."[74]

From the twelfth to the fourteenth centuries, with some gaps, the Manor was the possession of the Earls of Surrey (more commonly called Warenne). The thirteenth century records in this study are from the courts of the seventh Earl, John de Warenne, during 1274-75. His grandson John, the eighth Earl of Surrey, had "diverse bastards, and no lawful issue," so when he died in 1347, the lordship of the manor passed into the hands of the Crown.[75] However, the Earl's estranged widow Joan of Bar held dower lands in the Manor and continued to hold court as the Countess of Warenne for some years.[76] The later records in this study, 1350-1352, are from this period.

The manor has the distinction of having a nearly complete surviving series of court rolls from 1274 until the 1920s. These rolls contain records of court activity within the manor. During the thirteenth and fourteenth centuries, the manorial courts baron, usually held every three weeks,

---

[74] Watts, V. E., John Insley, and Margaret Gelling. *The Cambridge Dictionary of English Place-Names Based on the Collections of the English Place-Name Society,* p.644.

[75] Crowther, George H. *A Descriptive History of the Wakefield Battles; and a Short Account of This Ancient and Important Town,* p. 90.

[76] Habberjam p. xii.

dealt with civil litigation as well as the transfer of land and a variety of other civil issues.

The Rolls also contain records of the twice-yearly courts leet, called "tourn" here, in which the lord of the manor, through his representatives, enforced authority over issues such as brewing against the assize, bloodshed, debts, unjust raising of the hue and cry, and property damage.

The cases dealt with in the Wakefield manor courts were varied. In 1351, court was held in Wakefield on June 9, and this court included the following items, among others:

- Several men were found to have depastured the crops of others, and were amerced.
- William de Dounom was amerced 1d for a false trespassing claim against Thomas del Wroo. John de Fery and John Lene settled another trespassing claim.
- One debt plea was settled, while in another, Agnes who was the wife of Henry Souter was amerced for a false claim against William de Ayrmyn.
- Some tenants paid the lord for license to take or inherit land. Others surrendered land to be taken.[77]

A few weeks later, on July 25, a tourn court was held in Halifax. This court included the following items:

---

[77] Habberjam pp. 35-36.

- Several reports of people who "drew blood against the peace" and were amerced.
- Amercements were levied for obstructing common paths, brewing against the assize, and not coming to the tourn.

As in the manor court, pleas of debt (including false pleas) were also discussed in the tourn.[78] This court and tourn are fairly typical examples of the sort of material that is found in the thirteenth and fourteenth century Rolls.

---

[78] *Ibid.* pp. 42-45.

Four:

Classification of the Wakefield Names

For this study, names were drawn from the Wakefield Rolls during two periods: 1274-75 and 1350-52. The total names collected were 2,313, nearly evenly divided between the two periods: 1,148 from the 1270s and 1,165 from the 1350s. Women's names are a minority at 17% of the total names collected.

The thirteenth-century names were drawn from William Paley Baildon's 1901 edition of the Rolls. Baildon's translation of the names is fairly conservative, which can be verified by cross-checking with the Latin text that is included at the beginning of the book. (Sadly, later translators of the Rolls have not seen fit to include the Latin texts in their publications.) Baildon normalized many given names and tended to translate Latin occupational descriptives into English (for example, *Symon Prepositus de Hyperum* is translated as *Simon the Grave of Hipperholme*) but did not normalize names that were already in English form (*Thomas Undreclif* in the Latin text is also *Thomas Undreclif* in the translation, not *Undercliff*). When Baildon has translated a byname to English, I have cross-checked it in the Latin text and listed the Latin form in the Appendix, normalized to the nominative case if necessary.

On pages xviii-xix, Baildon discusses the problem of the "A *filius* W *de* B" name, such as *Adam filius Willelmi de Sandal*. Is this Adam William's son of Sandal, or Adam, son of William of Sandal? Baildon chose to consistently translate this type of name as the latter form, which is frequently confirmed within the text itself, and I have classified these names based on this sensible interpretation. In this example, *Adam filius Willelmi de Sandal* has a relationship byname: "son of William of Sandal," while William has a local byname: "of Sandal."

The fourteenth century names are drawn from the 1987 translation of the 1350-52 Rolls edited by Moira Habberjam, Mary O'Regan, and Brian Hale. Unfortunately, this edition does not include the Latin text of the Rolls, but the editors do discuss their editorial method as it relates to the translation of names. Local bynames are given with the spelling used in the Rolls, and surnames from occupations are also given as in the Rolls. They note that "this has the interesting corollary that unlike 1348-50 the present volume really has people called Smith and not Faber." This editorial method parallels Baildon's (like Baildon and most other editors of this type of material, they also normalize given names), and the names given in the 1350-52 volume appear to be trustworthy for the purposes of this study.

The vast majority of bynames in the combined data are either local names or relationship names; the two types together make up 76% of the names in this study (Fig. 1). Of the 2,313 names of persons in the combined data, 896 (38.7%) are local bynames, 862 (37.3%) are relationship bynames, 217 (9.4%) are occupational bynames, 190 (8.2%) are nicknames, 95 (4.1%) are unsure or "other," and 53 (2.3%) are given names only.

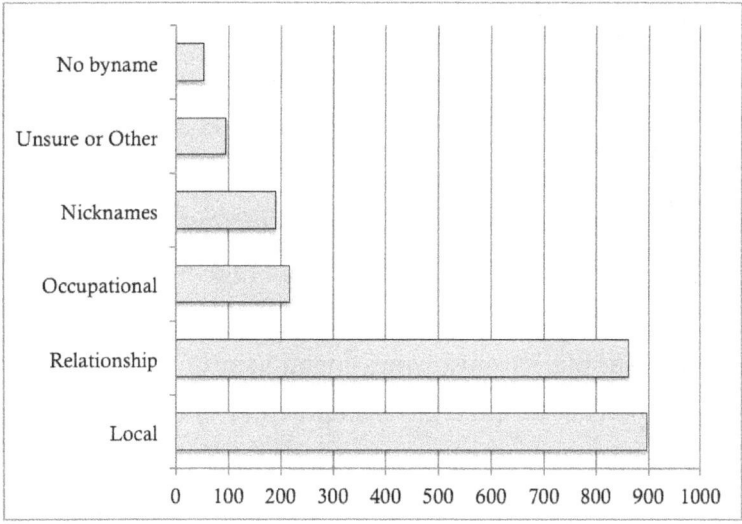

Fig. 1. Name types in the combined data.

Names of Relationship

Names indicating relationship were extremely common in the Wakefield Rolls. In the 1274-75 rolls, names of relationship made up 29% of the mentioned names. fifteen percent of the relationship bynames were borne by women.

The 1350-52 rolls show a significant increase in relationship bynames. These names make up a full 46% of the names in this period, and 34% of these relationship names belong to women.

Particularly common in the 1270s rolls is the *filius/filia* form: for example, *Robertus filius Anot, Willelmus filius Emme,* and *Sibilla filia Germani,* all from 1275. The modern translators of the rolls translate these names as *X son of/daughter of X,* with the exception of Baildon's translation of the knight *Willelmus filius Thome* as *William fitzThomas,* based on that family's later hereditary surname. These *filius/filia* forms make up a full 50% of the relationship names mentioned in these records: seventy percent of the relationship names in the 1270s, and decreasing to 38% of the 1350s relationship names.

A significant, consistent minority of relationship names are the "unmarked patronym/matronym" type, such as *John Alcok* or *Henry Elyot.* Of the relationship names in these records, 9.6% are of the unmarked type: 9.2% in the 1270s, and 9.9% in the 1350s.

Matronyms are a significant minority of names throughout this period, comprising 12.2% of the relationship names in this material: fifteen percent in the 1270s, and 10.4% in the 1350s. Whether the decrease in maternal relationships in these names between 1274 and 1350 is statistically relevant is not clear. It is possible that, as surnames began to become more important to one's identity masculine surnames may have been chosen because they had higher status, but this is only conjecture.

While names indicating son or daughter relationships are quite common, other relationships are also reflected in these bynames. Of the 1270s relationship names, 15.3% fall into this category, as do 20.7% of the 1350s relationship names. Parallel to the *filius/filia* names are names such as *Matilda uxor Johannis de Horton* "Matilda wife of John de Horton," *Agnes relicta Willelmi le Gardiner* "Agnes relict of William the Gardener," and *Willelmus frater Hugonis de Norlaund* "William the brother of Hugo de Norlaund." There is no indication that names of this type are hereditary; they appear to be purely descriptive. Other names such as *Adam Cusyn*, *Henry Urebrother* "our brother" and *Thomas Annotknave* contain non-parental relationship names in English instead of Latin; these might have been descriptive or hereditary.

There are at least some cases that appear to be hereditary relationship surnames. Redmonds, in *Names and History: People, Places and Things* discusses the case of the *Hebson* surname in the Wakefield Rolls.[79] Herbert de Butterley lived in the late thirteenth century. In the 1330s, we see *Thomas son of Richard son of Hebbe*, *Hebbe* being a diminutive form of *Herbert*. By 1350, Thomas is listed as *Thomas Hebson*, a likely victim of the Black Death whose daughter Alice is inheriting his land in Fulstone, and whose widow Agnes gives the lord 12d for license to remarry.[80] In Thomas' case, his *Hebson* surname does not refer to his father, but to his grandfather, so this is a case of a hereditary surname.

Local Names

Local bynames are very common during this period as well but seem to present a reverse pattern to that of relationship names. While relationship names grew from 29% of the 1270s total to 46% of the 1350s total, local names dropped from 44% of the 1270s names to 34% of the 1350s names. Women bore 7% of the local names in the 1270s, and 14% in the 1350s; this increase is probably indicative merely of the increase in women represented in the post-Black Death rolls.

Seventy percent of the local bynames in the rolls are the "de X" type, such as *Annabel de Fouleston*, *Jordan de Heppewrth*, or *Jacke de Yrland*. Most typically, "de X"

---

[79] Redmonds pp. 72-73.

[80] Walker p. 47, Jewell p. 229, Habberjam p. 15.

names refer to a village or farm in the general vicinity of Wakefield; villages represented in bynames include Alvirthorp (modern Alverthorpe), Hyperum (Hipperholme), Ossete (Ossett), Northuuerum (Northowram), Miggeley (Midgley) and many more. Other named places found in bynames include field names such as Eldwardholes and (probably) Thornetlay. It is quite likely that many of these names were not yet hereditary but only descriptive.

Most of the names refer to places that are identifiable today, and the rolls are a fertile source of early spellings of these place names. The vast majority are found in the Wakefield area, though some names represent places in Lancashire, Derbyshire, Warwickshire or even further afield. Some names reflect Continental origins, such as *Henry de Lascy* (Lassy, in Normandy) and *William de Loukes* (Liège, in Belgium). The name *John de Wales*, however, probably does not refer to the country of Wales, but instead to the West Riding place of the same name.

The remaining local names include "atte" names such as *Attewell, Attounend;* names referring to man-made structures such as *del Bothe* "of the cow-house," *del Brig* "of the bridge," or *del Halle*; and names referring to natural features such as *del Clyf, del Dene* "of the valley," *del Mire* "of the marsh," or *del Birkes* "of the birches."

Certain local names may bear some occupational meaning. For example, *del Bothe* or *del Bothes*, referring to a cow-shed, may be a name for a herdsman or cowman. However, it is difficult to determine whether these names are truly occupational, as they may also bear alternative meanings (for example, *del Bothe* may have meant that the name's bearer lived in a hovel).

Occupational Names

Occupational bynames in the Rolls represent a broad selection of medieval occupations. These names are not as common as one might expect, making up 9.4% of the total names in the study. Occupational names make a fairly consistent minority of names during this period: in the 1270s, 9.8% of names are occupational, and in the 1350s, 9.2% of names fall into this category. Though it is possible that some of these names may be hereditary and not descriptive, it seems likely that most are the latter, and the distribution of occupational bynames shows a clear picture of the type of work done in the manor.

The presence of women in this category changes from the thirteenth century to the fourteenth. Of the occupational names in the 1270s, 3.6% belong to women, while 15% of the occupational names in the 1350s are women's names. However, as with the other types of names in this study, this increase probably reflects nothing more than the increased number of women in the 1350s rolls.

The occupational names in these records include names that are both common and still clearly understood by modern English speakers, such as *Smith*, *Tayllour*,

Forester, and *Goldsmith*. Other names are more obscure to modern eyes. Names of this type include *Baly* "bailiff," *Jagger* "peddler or hawker," *Orfeour* "goldsmith or maker of gold embroidery," and *le Vacher*, a French name for a cow-herd, parallel to the also-present English byname *Couhird*.

The occupation type reflected most often in the Rolls is the craftsperson or skilled laborer. These make up 45.2% of the occupational names. Skilled craftspersons did many needed tasks for daily life in the manor, including building and working with wood or stone (*Carpenter*, *Hewere*, *Wright*), making small goods or hardware (*Chaundler* "candlemaker," *Couper* "barrelmaker," *Neyler* "nailmaker") and working with fabric, clothing or shoes (*Souter* "cobbler," *Lyster* "dyer," *Sewer*, *Taillour*, *Walker* "fuller of fabric," *Webester* "weaver"). A substantial subtype includes names related to the production or processing of food (*Bakur*, *Coke* "cook," *Mylner*).

The next-most common occupation types are the office or governing type and the manual labor type. The office or governing type includes 22.1% of the occupational names. These occupations were generally occupations of some particular authority in the manor, such as *Forester* or *Pynder* (the manor's animal control officer). Other examples include *Parker*, *Tollar* "toll-collector," and *Baly*. Names of the manual labor type make up 10.5% of the occupational names, including *Couhird*, *Ploghman*, and *Shephird*. Other occupational types make up the rest of the occupational byname stock, including clerical (*Clerk, Graffard*), commercial (*Chapman, Jagger, Mercer, Pedder*, all of these referring to types of merchants), entertainer (*Harpar, Pyper, Rymer*), and domestic (*Huswif, Wassher*).

The most common specific occupational names in the Rolls — *Grave, Milner, Smith, Clerk,* and *Forester* — provide further insight into common occupational roles in the manor. *Grave*, always given in the Latin form *Prepositus*, was the name for the office known elsewhere in England as the *reve* or *reeve*. Graves were bailiffs, elected each year from among the serfs. Among the grave's duties was to accept surrenders of land to the lord in court. There are 23 men listed in the 1274-75 rolls with the byname of *Prepositus*, e.g. *Symon Prepositus de Hyperum* "Simon, the grave of Hipperholme." At this stage it seems to be a purely descriptive name during the term of each person's graveship. Interestingly, we do not see *Prepositus* or *Grave* as a byname in the 1350s at all; in those records, graves are listed with other bynames (*e.g.* "John de Holway who was elected to the office of grave there..." or simply as "the grave," without a given name. This seems to imply that the elected graves in the 1270s did not have fixed surnames, and so *Prepositus* served as a functional descriptive byname, but by the 1350s the elected graves had surnames that were a stronger part of their identity, and so they would continue to be known by their existing surnames rather than replacing them with *Prepositus* or *Grave*.

Milner is a variant of *Miller*. The 1270s rolls invariably use the Latin *Molendinarius*, but the 1350s rolls use the English *Milner*, and this was the likely vernacular form in the thirteenth century as well. *Molendinarius* and *Milner* are found in these records 18 times. *Smith*, modernly the most common English surname, is also fairly frequent in the rolls, though in the earlier records it is found in its Latin form, *Faber*. *Faber* or *Smith* are found in these records 17 times. *Clerk* or its Latin translation *Clericus* is found in these records 16 times. The earlier forms are always Latin. *Forester* or the Latin *Forestarius* was a specialized task; the forester typically presented offenders against the Lord's timber or vert, although sometimes they performed other tasks as well. The name, in either English or Latin, appears in these records 13 times.

In comparison to these fairly common occupational names, most of which remain relatively common today, the Wakefield rolls also include names such as *Chaumpion*, *Henward*, *Hewere*, *Huswif*, *Paynter*, *Rymer*, *Wyndelester* "a windlass maker or seller," and *Queriour* "quarryman," that appear only once each.

At this stage it is difficult to find certain evidence of hereditary occupational surnames. If the bearer of an occupational surname follows that occupation, the name may be purely descriptive, but this is not certain. Roger *Pyper* is listed as a shoemaker and tanner – but in this case, that would not preclude him from being a piper as well, so this evidence says little. Another shoemaker and tanner is

Walter *Souter*, whose byname means "shoemaker," so like William *Salter*, who is listed as "a common forestaller of salt," the byname is likely descriptive.

Nicknames

Colorful but relatively uncommon, nicknames make up only 8.3% of the names in this study.

Nicknames are slightly more common in the earlier rolls, making 9.8% of the names in 1274-1275, with 5.4% of these borne by women. By the 1350s, nicknames are 7% of the listed names, with 11% of them borne by women. As above, the increase in women's names is probably attributable to the general increase in women listed in the rolls.

It is difficult to analyze these nicknames by type. While some of them are straightforward (*Fox*, for example, is clearly an animal nickname), others are less so (is *Godale* a phrase-type name for the hawker's phrase "Good ale!", or a metonym for what this person sold—or drank? Is *Hog* an animal nickname or a metonym for a swineherd?). For this reason, categorizing these nicknames can be a bit fuzzy, and some nicknames cannot be solidly categorized at all. Understanding this, one can still draw some conclusions from this data. The most common type of nickname is the "physical" type, referring to physical peculiarities such as hair, height, coloring, clothing, and the like. These names, including *Blunt* "blond," *Brun* "brown," *Grenehod* "green hood," and *Schort*, make up 23% of the nicknames.

Nicknames referring to animals, birds, and fish (such as *Bevere*, *Bulloc*, and *Wildgote*), those describing mental and moral characteristics (*Modisaule* "moody soul," *Theweles* "ill-mannered," and *Wyse*), and metonymic nicknames (*Ferthyng*, *Swerd*, and *Wytlof* "white loaf") are nearly equally represented in the rolls, the first two types being 17% of the total nicknames, and the last, 16%.

Oath- or phrase-type nicknames are rare in this data; there are only three that seem relatively possible to belong in that category: *Pes* "peace," *Goye* "joy," and *Godale* "good ale." Obscene names, despite the renowned Middle English lack of delicacy in such matters, are even rarer. There is only one name with a possible obscene meaning, and even this is uncertain: *Ters*, which may mean "third son," but may also mean "penis."

Five:

Names in their time

A closer examination of the Wakefield names, when categorized by their date, illuminates changes during the roughly 75-year period between the earliest and latest names.

Though local and relationship bynames are nearly equally distributed when considered in the context of the combined data, there is a noticeable change in distribution of names of this type from the 1270s to the 1350s, as seen in figures 2, 3, and 4. Local names are the most common in the thirteenth century Rolls, while relationship names are the most common in the mid-fourteenth century records.

Other name types decrease somewhat in popularity during this period. Nicknames show a noticeable decrease, from 9.5% in the 1270s to 6.7% in the 1350s. Nicknames are a minority in each period, but the decrease may be an indication of a certain increased formality of bynames as they developed into fixed surnames during the fourteenth century. The increased use and sense of identity of these names would have made the informal playful nickname based on an item of clothing or a physical quirk both less useful and perhaps less desired. Nicknames tend to be given by others, not assumed by the bearer, but once the bearer begins to self-identify by a name, particularly for any sort of official purpose, nicknames with unwanted or frivolous meanings could fall by the wayside.

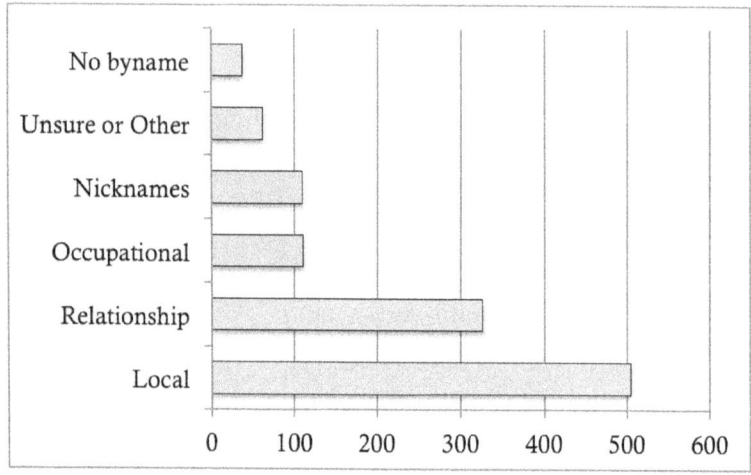

Fig. 2. Name Types in 1274-1275.

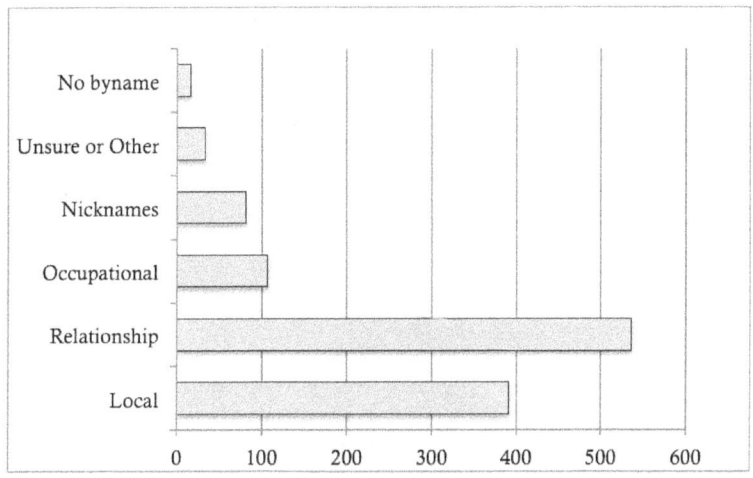

Fig. 3. Name Types in 1350-1352.

Further indication of the spread of surnames is that people listed in the Rolls with no byname at all decrease from 3.2% of the 1270s names, some of whom are clearly commonly known by a single name (Pouwe, as an example, is mentioned several times with no byname, in contexts where others are listed with bynames) to 1.4% of the 1350s names, nearly all of whom are merely referred to in passing as someone's parent or other relative, and thus may actually have had a byname that was not mentioned in this context.

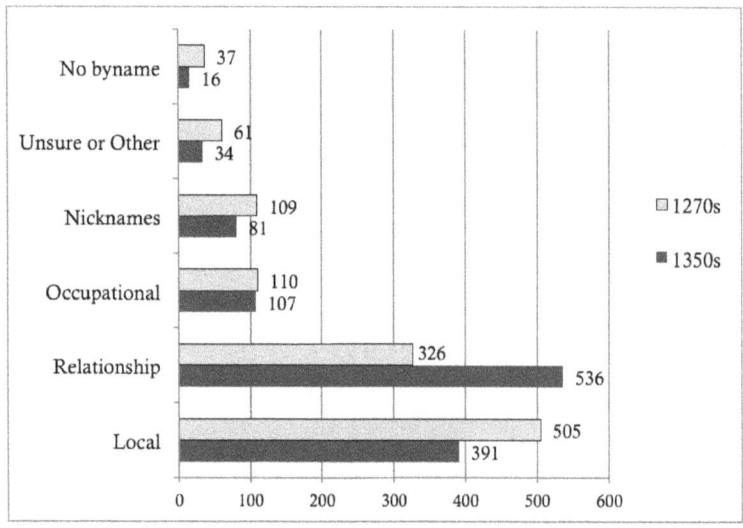

Fig. 4. Changing Name Types from 1270s-1350s.

1274-1275: An Overview

As mentioned earlier, the most common type of byname in the 1270s Rolls is the local byname, such as de Eldwardeholes, del Grene, or de Hudresfeld. These names reflect villages, fields, woods, and other natural landmarks, most of which are in or around the Manor.

Relationship names in this period are almost entirely of the filius/filia type, and typically appear to be descriptive of the bearer's actual relationships.

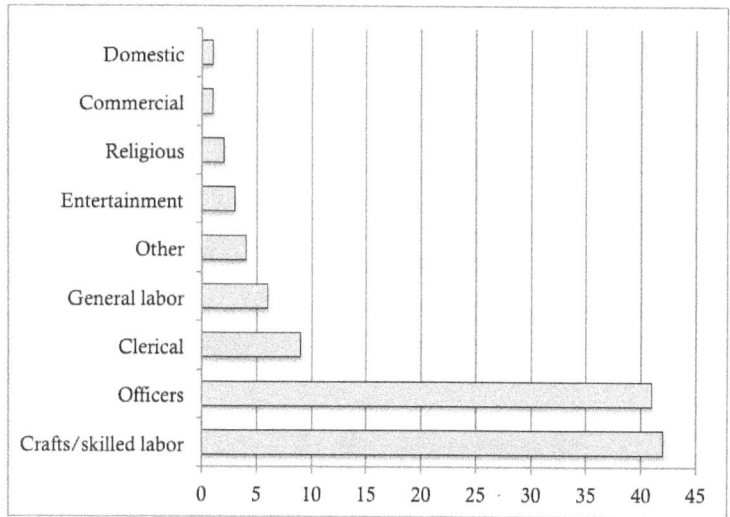

Fig. 5. Occupational Names, 1270s.

The majority of occupational bynames in the 1270s fall mostly into two categories: craftspersons and skilled laborers, and officers (Fig. 5). Craftpersons' bynames in this period are frequently, but not always, written in Latin: e.g. Alcok Carpentarius, Willelmus Sutor, Rogerus Fullo. However, there are examples recorded in English as well: Henry le Hewere, Richard le Neyler, Elias le Tynker de Sourby.

Officers' names are very common in this period, but this is the result of one particular office description, that of the grave. Holders of this office were typically called by the byname Prepositus while they held the office, or when referring to previous activity in that office, but this name was not used outside of that context.

The distribution of nicknames in the 1270s names is fairly evenly spread among five categories: the most common being physical nicknames such as Schort, followed by "other" names that are difficult to categorize, metonyms such as Wytlof, animal nicknames such as Bulloc, and mental/emotional "personality" nicknames such as Modisaule (Fig. 6).

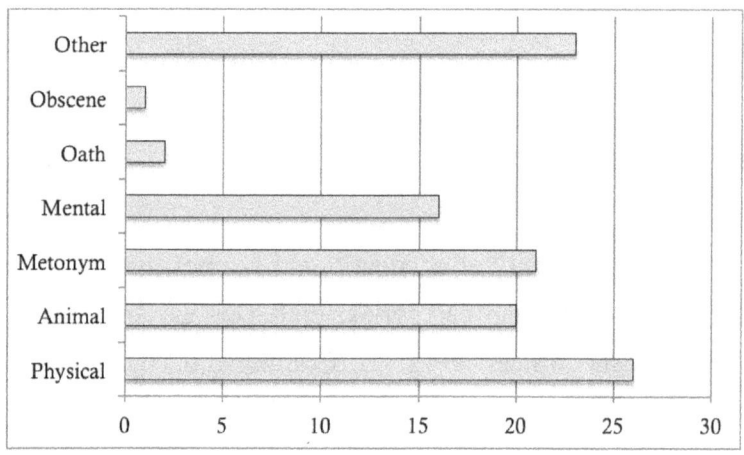

Fig. 6. Nicknames, 1270s.

1350-1352: An Overview

In contrast to the 1270s names, in which local bynames were the most common type, the most common type of byname in the 1350s Rolls is the relationship byname, such as Dobson, Hughdoghter, or Nicolknave. As mentioned earlier, these are most commonly referring to parent/child relationships but also include other types of relationships.

A notable change in the 1350s names is the new prominence of names of the X-son/X-daughter form, such as Adam Jordanson and Margery Juddoghter. These names are simply not found in the 1270s records, with one exception: Thomas Sampson, attorney to Sir Geoffrey de Neville. It is possible that the names were used in the vernacular, but were not written as such in the Latin documents, or that they were not used at all. In A Dictionary of English Surnames, Reaney suggests that –son forms were in use throughout this period, and that fourteenth century scribes simply tended to be more likely to record the vernacular instead of translating it into Latin (xx). The increase in –son names during the middle 1300s is also seen in other Yorkshire records (li). In the 1350s rolls, names of this type make up 31% of all relationship bynames.

An interesting variation of these names is the double patronym type (in some cases, including a matronym), such as Thomas Jonson Dobson "Thomas the son of John the son of Dobbe," or Robert Jonson Emmot "Robert the son of John the son of Emmot (Emma)." This name pattern appears 12 times in the 1350s rolls, making 2% of the relationship names there.

It is not clear why there was such an increase in the use of relationship names between 1275 and 1350. What does seem clear is that names in Yorkshire were still in flux at this time, and a parent with a local surname might have a child with a relationship name, or vice versa. Perhaps relationship names simply became more fashionable during this time. Another possibility is that, as the population grew, and the choices of given names became less diverse during the fourteenth century, relationship names did a better job of distinguishing people than many local names might have. If there were two Adams from Halifax, calling both Adam de Halifax would not be as functional as calling one Adam Jonson and the other Adam Emmotson. However, there were certainly other ways to differentiate the two Adams (including nicknames and occupational bynames), so this does not fully explain the increase in popularity of relationship names.

There is a noticeable difference in the distribution of occupational names in the 1350s, compared to the earlier period. The percentage of bynames referring to skilled craftspersons such as Chaundler, Smith or Tayllour has risen, and now makes up over half of the occupational names (Fig. 7). The officers' names, on the other hand, have nearly disappeared. The disappearance of these types of names is primarily the result of the disappearance of "grave/prepositus" as a primary byname for those serving in that office.

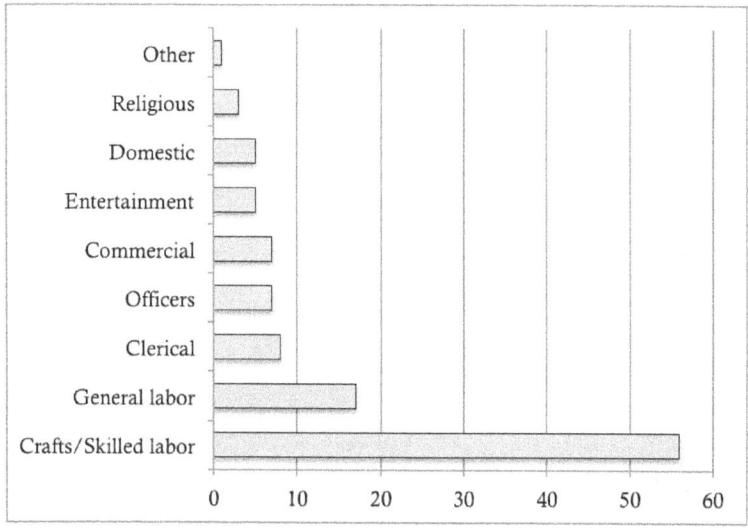

Fig. 7. Occupational Names, 1350s.

General labor bynames such as Shephird and Hayward are slightly more common in this period, while other types of occupational names do not seem to show a statistically relevant increase or decrease.

As mentioned earlier, there is a decrease in nickname bynames from the 1270s to this period. However, of the recorded nicknames we do see in the 1350s, the distribution of nickname types remains fairly consistent from that in the 1270s (Fig. 8). The nickname type that shows the largest change is the metonymic type, which drops from 21 names in the 1270s to 11 names in the 1350s; however, the sample size is small enough that it is not possible to tell whether this change is significant.

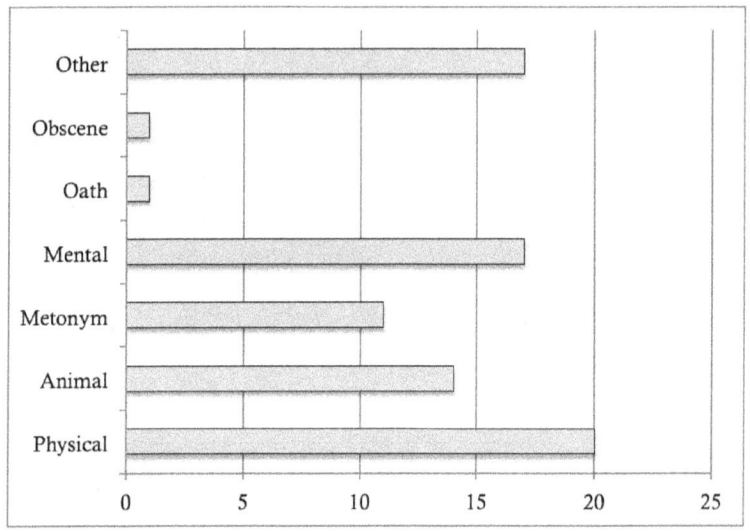

Fig. 8. Nicknames, 1350s.

Six:

Conclusions

Surnames at this point were still frequently literal and descriptive, and as such they tell us more about the people who bore them than modern surnames would. The most common ways to describe people, based on the names in the Wakefield Rolls, were where they lived and to whom they were connected. This is quite similar to modern informal naming processes: "I'm sure you've met the guy before. It's Joe from Tacoma/Joe, Ann's brother." This gives us a sense of how people, then as now, felt "in place" in their society and tended to bear an identity based on their position in the social structure and their physical location in the community.

Locative bynames in the Rolls are mostly local West Riding places, which as one might expect, indicates a less mobile society than that to which modern people are accustomed. However, there is a minority of names from further afield, evidence of some level of mobility.

Relationship bynames in the Rolls are mostly "son of/daughter of/wife of *X* (male)" names, but what is notable in the Wakefield names is the number of matronymic bynames, which might be expected to be more rare. It is sometimes assumed that these names are used in cases of bastardy, but there is no clear evidence of illegitimacy in the majority of these names in the Rolls studied.

Occupational names show a good cross-section of the occupations carried out in the manor, particularly by the skilled craftspeople whose identity would definitely have been based on what they did. Craftspeoples' skills would be highly valued and thus a craftperson's identity as an artisan would distinguish him or her more strongly than place or relationship would.

Wakefield people could be blunt and whimsical, as seen in the nicknames they gave. These give us, perhaps, the most illuminating glance into the late medieval English mind. While straightforward nicknames based on the bearer's physical attributes were common, we see a fair number of names that are metaphorical, including the common metonymic bynames. Uncomplimentary names are found as well, indicating that these people did not necessarily pull punches when naming each other. Modern people do not either, but they generally do not use uncomplimentary names in official contexts; such names are informal, and people bearing uncomplimentary hereditary surnames often change them, if the name wasn't already changed for that reason by an ancestor.

The Wakefield Rolls give us a good, if slightly impressionistic, view of the lives of people in late-medieval West Yorkshire during the period of surname development. We see a people who were firmly woven into the fabric of their West Riding community, and whose names demonstrate the relationships, homes, work, attitudes, and actions that defined their lives. Though our more mobile and fractured modern society differs in many ways from that of the medieval Yorkshire folk, the attributes reflected in Wakefield names demonstrate constants of human lives that have changed very little in the intervening seven centuries.

Seven:

The names

Latin names have been normalized to the nominative form. Surnames are not normalized unless noted, and are given in Latin if that was the form used. Place names are in Yorkshire unless otherwise noted. Latin bynames are listed under their English translation, which is marked with a + if unattested in this collection of names.

Header forms are the most common form in the attested names; when this is not definitive, the header form is generally the earliest form, however, there are some exceptions (for example, *Irland* rather than *Yreland*) to place names under a header form that seemed more logical.

Abbreviations in this listing:
V1: Baildon, *Court Rolls of the Manor of Wakefield*
V6: Habberjam et. al., *Court Rolls of the Manor of Wakefield*
MED: *The Middle English Dictionary*

OED: *The Oxford English Dictionary*
Reaney: *A Dictionary of English Surnames*, unless otherwise noted.
Smith: *The Place Names of the West Riding of Yorkshire*, listed by volume and page, so "Smith vi.183" is from page 183 of volume VI of *The Place Names of the West Riding*. Other references in this appendix may be easily found in the bibliography section of this work.
+ : Normalized English form of a Latin byname
(f): Female
ME: Middle English
OE: Old English
OF: Old French
ON: Old Norse
OWScand: Old West Scandinavian
s.n., s.v.: *sub nomen*, "under the name"; *sub verbum*, "under the word"

LOCATIVE SURNAMES

Abbay
"One who lives or works at the abbey." From OF *abeie*. (Reaney s.n. Abbay, MED s.v. abbeie (n.))
    Thomas del Abbey 1350 V6 p11

Acreland
Modern Acreland. OE *æcer* "a plot of arable land" + *land* "land, tract of land, district, strip of land in the common field." (Smith vi.183)

Simon Acreland 1350 V6 p3
Adam Acreland 1351 V6 p38

Aderichegate
Modern Addersgate in Northowram. From OE personal name *Æþelric* or *Eadric* + ON *gata*, "road." (Smith iii.97)
Robert de Aderichegate 1350 V6 p8

Aldewrth
Modern Holdsworth. The meaning is "Halda's enclosure" from OE personal name *Halda* + *worþ* "enclosure." (Smith iii.114)
Bate de Aldewrth 1275 V1 p111
John de Aldewrth 1275 V1 p111 "de eadem"

Aldonlay
Modern Aldonley is a housing estate in West Yorkshire, within Almondbury and Huddersfield, probably on the same site as the medieval Aldonley. Aldonley appeared in records from 1336 to the 18th century. (Redmonds, *English Surnames* 173)
Alice de Aldonlay, Aldounlay (f) 1352 V6 p96, 99

Almanbiry
Modern Almondbury. "Fortified place owned or maintained by the men of the village," from the dative form of ON *almenn* + OE *byrig*, dative singular of *burh*. (Watts s.n. Almondbury)
Adam de Almanbiry 1274 V1 p97

Alstanley
Modern Austonley. "Alstan's glade or clearing," from the OE personal name *Ælfstan* or *Alhstan* + *lēah*. (Smith ii.263)

Gilbert de Alstanley 1274 V1 p98
Richard de Alstanley 1274 V1 p98
Gamel de Alstanley 1275 V1 p118
William de Alstanley 1275 V1 p119
Henry de Alstonlay, Altonlay 1350 V6 p9, 80

Alvirthorpe
Modern Alverthorpe. "Ælfhere's outlying farmstead," from the OE personal name *Ælfhere* + ON *þorp* "farmstead." (Ekwall ODEPN s.n. Alverthorpe; Smith ii.166)
    Adam de Alverthorpe, Alvirthorp 1274 V1 p84, 102
    Philip de Alvirthorp, Alvirthorpe 1274 V1 p101, 131
    Richard de Alvirthorpe 1274 V1 p84
    Gerbot de Alvirthorpe, Alvirthorp 1274 V1 p83, 84, 85, 88, 108 Frequently referred to in these records as simply "Gerbot" (106, for example)

Amyas
From Amiens. (Reaney s.n. Amias)
    John de Amyas 1351 V6 p66

Apelyerd
Appleyard is a lost place in the West Riding, meaning "apple orchard" from OE *æppel* + *geard*. (Reaney s.n. Appleyard, Smith i.341)
    Elyas del Apelyerd 1275 V1 p147

Asberne
Probably a place named from OE *Ashburn* "ash-tree stream." (Watts s.nn. Ashburnham Place, Ashburton)
    John de Asberne 1274 V1 p94

Astey

Modern Ashday. Smith suggests the name originates from OE *ēast* "east" + OE *ge(hæg)* "enclosure" or **hēah* "a height." I am not sure whether *Hastey* is the same place, but I have been unable to find another source of that name, and the *a/h* alternation is not unheard of in this context. (Smith iii.90)

    William de Astey 1275 V1 p115
    Adam de Hastey 1275 V1 p115
    Gilbert de Hasteye 1275 V1 p124

Attewelle

"A dweller by the well (stream or spring)." (Reaney s.n. Attwell)

    Adam Attewelle 1351 V6 p38

Attoun

"One who lives at the town." (Reaney s.n. Town, which also cites *Inthetune*, *above the toune*, and *Douninthetoune*.)

    Thomas Attoun 1350 V6 p12

Attounend

"One who lives at the town's end." In the fourteenth century we start to see this name in various English forms, but in the thirteenth century Rolls it was commonly in Latin, as *ad capud ville*. (Reaney s.n. Townend)

    Johannes ad capud ville de Soureby 1274 V1 p22
    Henricus ad capud ville 1275 V1 p41, 71
    Richard Attounend 1351 V6 p67

Avoden

The *-den* element here probably means "valley," from OE *denu* (c.f. Ovenden, Alcomden in Smith), but I cannot find the place name associated with this.

Juliana de Avoden (f) 1351 V6 p18
Nicholas de Avoden 1351 V6 p17, 105
Cecilia de Avoden (f) 1352 V6 p102

Aynesford
I have not found this name in the West Riding, but there is an Eynsford in Kent which would have been written similarly. It means "Ægen's ford," from the OE personal name *Ægen* (in the genitive form) + *ford*. (Watts s.n. Eynsford)
William de Aynesford 1275 V1 p137

Ayrmyn
Airmyn is quite a bit east of Wakefield. The name means "mouth of the river Aire," with ON *mynni*. (Watts s.n. Airmyn, Smith ii.13)
William de Ayrmyn 1351 V6 p31, 33

Bairstowe
The element -*stow* in place names generally means "place." In this case, "place where berries grew," from OE *beger* "berry" and *stow* "place." There were two Bairstows; one is in Sowerby Bridge, and one is now lost but was in Southowram. (Smith iii.141, 90)
Johanna de Bairstow, Bairstowe, Bairstawe (f) 1350
    V6 p12, 79, 82
Richard de Bairstowe 1350 V6 p6

Bar⁺
A bar is an obstruction or barrier; typically a gate. (Reaney s.n. Barr, MED s.v. barre)
Alicia ad Barram (f) 1274 V1 p8, 50

Barkeshere

Baildon, in his index, equates this name with modern Barsey, which in this period was spelled in ways including *Barkeshey, Barkissey*, etc. The name means "Bark's enclosure," from the ON personal name *Barkr* or *Bǫrkr* + OE *(ge)hæg*. See Barkesland, below. (Smith iii.58, 57)

    Hugh de Barkeshere 1274 V1 p94

Barkesland

Modern Barkisland. "Bark's cultivated land," from the ON personal name *Barkr* or *Bǫrkr* + OE *land*. See Barkeshere, above. (Smith iii.57, Watts s.n. Barkisland)

    John de Barkesland 1275 V1 p124
    William de Barkesland 1275 V1 p155
    Thomas of Berkesland 1352 V6 p69

Barn

Probably "of the barn." (MED s.v. bern, Reaney s.n. Barne)

    John del Barm or Barn 1274 V1 p81

Barneby

Probably Barmby or Barnby, both Yorkshire place names. (Ekwall ODEPN s.nn. Barmby on the Marsh, Barnby Moor; Smith vii.8,9)

    William de Barneby 1274 V1 p86
    Richard de Barm' 1275 V1 p115

Barnedeside

Modern Barnside, in Hepworth. "Burnt hillside," from OE *berned* + *sīde*. (Smith ii.243)

    Elias del Barnedeside, Barneside 1274 V1 p82

Bately
Modern Batley, NW of Wakefield. "Bata's forest-glade," from OE personal name *Bata* + *lēah*. (Smith ii.179, Mills s.n. Batley)
    John de Bately 1274 V1 p83, 84
    Richard de Bately, Bateley 1274 V1 p83, 144
    William de Bateley 1275 V1 p144

Baugecler
This is probably locative but I cannot find a certain place name for this. Modern Burghclere is about 200 miles away, in Hampshire, and doesn't show period forms that parallel this form, so it is an unlikely origin for this name. However, the name may be similar; *-cler* is possibly ME *clēr*, meaning "a forest-glade, a clearing." (MED s.v. clēr (n.), Watts s.n. Burghclere)
    Elias Baugecler, de Baugecler 1274 V1 p83, 85, 86
    Alice wife of /widow of Baugecler, Elias de Baugecler (f) 1275 V1 p111. "Wife of Baugecler" is an unusual use of a locative name in these records: *Alicia uxor Baugecler*.

Bentlay
Modern Bentley. "Clearing where bent grass grows," from OE *beonet* + *lēah*. Smith suggests that the modern Bentley in West Yorkshire is identical to the place called Benclyfe in the fourteenth century. But as this surname is also fourteenth century, one wonders. (Watts s.n. Bentley, Smith iii.243)
    Henry de Bentlay 1352 V6 p69

Bentlayrod
Modern Bentley Royd. "Forest clearing overgrown with bent-grass." (Smith iii.145)

Adam del, de Bentlayrod, Bentlayrode 1351 V6 p33, 55, 93

Berdeshill
Possibly a modern Birdshill, but I have not been able to find this location.
Robert de Berdeshill 1352 V6 p96

Bir'
It is unclear what this place name might be. Several names are possible, e.g. East and North Bierley, or see also Byry.
Henry de Bir' 1275 V1 p123

Birkenschawe
Modern Birkenshaw. "Birchen wood," from OE *bircen* + *sceaga*, "wood." The *k* in *Birken*- is from ON influence, which is not uncommon in this region. (Smith iii.13).
William del Birkenschawe 1274 V1 p93
Thomas de Birkynschagh 1351 V6 p23

Birkes
"Of/by the birches." (Reaney, s.n. Birks; MED s.v. birch(e))
Richard del Birkes 1275 V1 p118

Birstall
Modern Birstall, "the site of a fort," from OE *byrh-stall*. (Smith iii.14, Mills s.n. Birstall)
John de Birstall, Birstal, Byrstal 1275 v1 p83, 87, 102, 132, 136
Richard de Birstall 1350 V6 p8

Birton
There are multiple places in Yorkshire that are modernly spelled "Burton", but this is probably modern Kirkburton. From OE *byrh* + *tūn*, "a fortified enclosure." (Smith ii.245, Watts s.nn. Burton, Kirkburton)
 William de Birton 1274 V1 p84, 143
 John de Birton, Byrton 1275 V1 p139, 146
 Robert de Birton 1351 V6 p17

Botham
Possibly modern Bootham, also a name meaning "at the booths," from OWScand *búð, -um*. (Smith 1-13).
 William del Botham, Bothom 1350 V6 p5, 14

Bothemley
Modern Bottomley, near Halifax. "Clearing in the valley bottom," from OE *botm* (or *boðm*) + *lēah*. (Reaney s.n. Bottomley, Smith iii.58)
 Hugh de Bothemley 1275 V1 p124

Botherode
Modern Boothroyd, near Rastrick. *-royd* is a common name element in Yorkshire. In this case, the name means "a clearing with a booth or shed" from OE *bōth* + *rod*. (Smith iii.38)
 Adam del Botherode 1274 V1 p80
 Gilbert de Bouderode, Bouderod 1274 V1 p87
 John del Botherode 1274 V1 p80
 Margery de Bouderod (f) 1275 V1 p91
 Thomas de Bouderode 1275 V1 p106
 John del Botherode 1350 V6 p16
 John de Botherod 1351 V6 p20
 John de Boudrod 1351 V6 p46
 William Boudrod 1352 V6 p88

Bothe, Bothes

Probably "of the cow-house or herdman's hut"; a name for a cowman or herdsman, or referring to another type of hut or hovel. ME *bōþ(e)* from Old Danish *bōth*. (Reaney s.n. Booth, MED s.v. bōth (n.))

    Gilbert del Bothes 1274 V1 p81
    Bate del Bothes 1275 V1 p113, 116 also listed on p116 as "Bate son of Hugh del Bothes"
    Hugh de, del Bothes 1275 V1 p116
    Simon de Bothes 1275 V1 p110 probably the same as Simon the Grave of Bothes, p111
    Robert de, del Bothe 1350 V6 p2, 4, 46 (same as Robert del Bothes?)
    Adam del Bothe 1351 V6 p17
    Gilbert Bothe, del Bothe 1351 V6 p18, 80
    Robert del Bothes 1351 V6 p52 (same as Robert del Bothe?)
    William del Bothe 1351 V6 p17, 19
    Alice del Both (f) 1352 V6 p92 servant
    Eglent del Bothes 1352 V6 p75
    Thomas del Bothe 1352 V6 p73

Bothstede

Modern Booth Stead. The name means "the shed site," from ODan *bōth* + OE *stede*. (Smith iii.123)

    Adam del Bothstede 1352 V6 p93

Bothun

Bothun or *bothen* was a word for certain plants, including rosemary and corn marigold. This could be a locative name for one who lived or worked around such plants. It could also be an error for "bottom," which was sometimes spelled similarly as *bothen,* and would refer to someone who lived

at the bottom of a valley. (MED s.vv. bothen (n.), botme (n.); Smith iii.111)
    Agnes del Bothun (f) 1275 V1 p136

Bourgh
Bourgh is "a city, a town, a small village"; another form, *Burgo*, is a Latin version. It is a common place name element from one of many place names called *Burgh*, meaning a town, a city, and particularly, a chartered borough. (Reaney s.nn. Burk, Burgh; MED s.v. burgh (n. (1)))
    Thomas de Burgo 1274 V1 p83 87
    Amice del Bourgh (f) 1350 V6 p4

Brad
Were this *le* and not *del*, this would probably be a nickname meaning "Richard the Broad (large, fat)." The *del* makes this more likely to be a locative or occupational name, but I cannot pinpoint which one. *Brad* was a common element in place names meaning "wide, open," and there are several in the area such as Bradford, Bradley, etc. (MED s.vv. brōd (n.(3)), brōd (adj.))
    Richard del Brad 1350 V6 p4

Bradeley
Modern Bradley. A common West Yorkshire place name from an OE compound, *brād* + *lēah*, meaning "broad clearing." (Smith iii.49)
    William de Bradeley 1275 V1 p112
    William de Bradelay, Bradeley 1350 V6 p5, 7

Brampton
Modern Brampton Bierlow or Brampton en le Morthen. "Farmstead where broom grows," from OE *brōm* + *tūn*.

(Ekwall ODEPN s.n. Brampton, Reaney s.n. Brampton, Smith i.106, 162)
    Thomas de Brampton 1350 V6 p2

Brathewell
Modern Braithwell. According to Ekwall, this is "a Scandinavianized form of Bradwell," so the meaning is "broad well or stream." From OE *brād* + *wella*, influenced by the ON cognate *breiðr*. (Ekwall ODEPN s.nn. Braithwell, Bradwell; Smith i.132)
    John de Brathewell 1352 V6 p82

Brerley
Modern Brearley. A "clearing amongst or overgrown with briars," OE *brēr* + *lēah*. (Smith iii.159)
    Roger de Brerley, Brereley 1275 V1 p117, 141, 146
        (the serjeant of Tymberwode)

Bretton
From one of two places in the West Riding, either Monk Bretton or West Bretton. OE "farmstead of the Britons," from the genitive plural form of *Brettas* + *tūn*. (Watts s.n. Bretton; Smith ii.99, i.273)
    Richard de Bretton 1274 V1 p100, 132
    John de Bretton 1275 V1 p127
    Luvecok de Bretton 1275 V1 p123
    Peter de Bretton 1275 V1 p123
    Swayn de Bretton 1275 V1 p145

Brickhouses
Brighouse (see Brighous, below) is a nearby place name meaning "houses by the bridge," but this spelling seems perhaps to be a different word; none of the cited forms of Brighouse in Smith contain a *c* or a *k*. "Brick," the building

material, is a word borrowed from Middle Dutch *bricke*, and not typically spelled this way in Middle English. The word *Brickhouse* is also a nearby place name, but It is not cited in Smith until the 19th century. (Smith iii.76, 2 193; MED s.v. brike (n. (1)))

    John del Brickhouses 1275 V1 p111

Bridelington
Modern Bridlington. "Estate called after Brehtel," from the OE personal name **Brehtel + ing + tūn*. (Watts s.n. Bridlington)

    William de Bridelington 1275 V1 p130

Brig
"One who lives by the bridge." (Reaney s.n. Brigg)
    Robert del Brig of Stanesfeld 1275 V1 p116
    Richard del Brig, Brigg 1350 V6 p2 , 55
    Robert del Brig, Brigg 1350 V6 p2, 55
    Roger del Brig 1350 V6 p4
    William del Brig 1351 V6 p20
    Gilbert del Brig 1352 V6 p71
    John del Brig 1352 V6 p71

Brighous
Brighouse is a nearby place name meaning "houses by the bridge." From OE *brycg + hūs*. (Smith iii.76)
    Richard de Briggehuses 1275 V1 p105
    Susannah del Brighuses (f) 1275 V1 p148
    Adam del Brighous 1352 V6 p72
    John del Brighous senior 1352 V6 p89

Brocheles
Modern Brock Holes, meaning "badger holes," and a common name in the West Riding. From OE *brocc* + *hol*. (Smith ii.272)
    Richard de Brocheles, Brocholis 1275 V1 p120

Brodbothem
Modern Broad Bottom, meaning "broad valley bottom." From OE *brād* + *boðm*. (Smith iii.159)
    Alan de Brodbothem 1275 V1 p126
    John del Brodbothem 1275 V1 p126
    Adam del Brodbothem, de Brodebothem 1275 V1
        p126, 153

Brodheved
"Dweller by the broad headland." The *de* indicates that It is probably a locative rather than a nickname "broad head." (Reaney s.n. Broadhead)
    Richard de Brodheved 1350 V6 p2

Brounhill
"Brown Hill," of which there are several in West Yorkshire, or a more generic "dweller by the brown hill." (Smith viii.26, Reaney s.n. Brownell)
    John del Brounhill 1350 V6 p15
    Adam del Brounhill 1352 V6 p105

Buterle
Modern Butterley. "Clearing with rich, butter-producing pasture," from OE *butere* + *lēah*. (Smith ii.239)
    Adam de Buttreley 1274 V1 p98
    William de Buttreley, Buterle 1274 V1 p98, 118
    Herbert de Butterley, Buterle 1275 V1 p119, 120 (This
        Herbert, also called Hebbe, is the ancestor of the

later Hebson family (see Thomas Hebson in this record). (Smith ii.239, Redmonds N&H 72))
   Roger de Buterle 1275 V1 p118
   Thomas de Boterlay 1351 V6 p59
   Thomas de Butirlay 1351 V6 p18

Bynglay
Modern Bingley. Probably "the clearing of the Binningas, the people called after Bynni," from the OE folk name *Bynningas* + *lēah*, but possibly "a clearing with a heap or a hollow" from OE *bing* + *lēah*. (Watts s.n. Bingley)
   William de Bynglay 1351 V6 p61

Byry
Possibly "servant at the manor house," or "one employed at the cow house." (Reaney s.nn. Byars, Berry)
   Henry de Byry, Byrry 1275 V1 p137, 144
   John de Byre, Byry 1351 V6 p42, 43, 72

Bythebrok
"By the brook," one who lives near a brook. (Reaney s.n. Brook)
   Henry Bythebrok 1350 V6 p8

Bythestonhirst
"By the stoney hill." *Hirst* or *hurst* can mean a hill, or a grove. (MED s.v. hirst(e)
   Adam del Bythestonhirst 1352 V6 p73

Bythesyk
Syk is from OE *sīc* or ON *sík*, meaning a "small stream or ditch," so this name means "one who lives by the stream." There are several place names in West Yorkshire still

containing this name element. (Smith vii.243)
    John Bythesyk 1352 V6 p89

Canford
Presumably this is from a place that would modernly be called Canford. I have been unable to find one in Yorkshire, though there is one in Dorset. This could be from that place, or a now lost place name, from the OE personal name *Cana + ford*. (Watts s.n. Canford Cliffs)
    Thomas de Canford 1351 V6 p67

Cartewrth
Modern Cartworth. "Cræta's enclosure," from the OE personal name *Cræta + worð*. (Smith ii.236)
    Roger de Cartewrth 1274 V1 p98
    Adam de Cartewrth 1275 V1 p121
    Thomas de Cartewrth 1275 V1 p106

Castelford
Modern Castleford. The "castle" element is actually OE *ceaster*, so the name means "ford near the fortification," from OE *ceaster + ford*. (Reaney s.n. Castleford, Smith ii.69)
    Richard de Castelford 1274 V1 p86
    William de Castelford 1275 V1 p132
    Richard de Castilf(ord?) 1275 V1 p130
    Philip de Castelford 1351 V6 p36, 103

Castell
One who lives near or is employed at a castle; possibly one who owes services or rent to a castle. *de Castello* is a Latinized version in the earlier Rolls; the surnames de Castel, del Castel, and del Castell appear in fourteenth century editions of the Rolls. (Reaney s.n. Castle,

Castlehow; Sheridan Walker, *Wakefield Court Rolls 1331-1333*, p114, 133; v6 p9)
    Agnes de Castello (f) 1274 V1 p91
    William del Castell 1350 V6 p9

Caylly
From Cailly in Normandy. (Reaney s.n. Caley)
    John de Caylly, Kaylli 1274 V1 p83, 107

Chapel⁺
One who resides near or works at a chapel. (Reaney s.n. Chappel)
    Robertus de Capella 1275 V1 p118, 148

Chayley
There is a modern "Shaley" in the area, but etymologically, the form "Chayley" doesn't quite fit during this period. Fourteenth century spellings in the WCR are commonly *Shaghlay* or *Schaghlay*, though in the 15th C we see *Chaglayhous*. There is also a Chailey in Sussex, but during this period it was spelled *Chaggeleye*, *Chaggelegh*, *Chaggelye*, etc. (Smith ii.254, Ekwall ODEPN s.n. Chailey, Watts s.n. Chailey)
    Thomas de Chayley 1350 V6 p2

Cheet
Possibly modern Chevet; Smith cites spellings such as *Chete*, *Chet* starting in 1377, and *Cheet(e)* from 1530. If this is indeed the source, the name may mean "the ridge," akin to Welsh *cefn* "back, ridge." (See also Chyvet, below.) (Smith i.278)
    Thomas de Cheet 1351 V6 p52

Cheswaldlay

The Cheswold is a nearby river. *-lay* is probably from OE *lēah*, "a wood or clearing in a wood," so this is "a clearing near the Cheswold." (Smith vii.122, 219)

    John de Cheswaldlay 1350 V6 p11
    Margery de Cheswaldlay (f) 1352 V6 p91

Chorlton

From Chorlton, in Lancashire. (Reaney s.n. Chorlton)

    Thomas de Chorlton 1351 V6 p50

Chydeshyll

Modern Chidswell. "Cid's Hill," from an OE personal name **Cid(d)* + *hyll*. (Smith ii.196)

    Henry de Chydeshyll 1275 V1 p108

Chyvet

Modern Chevet. The origin seems to be uncertain, but Smith suggests that it is from Welsh *cefn* "back, ridge." (Smith vii.84-85, i.278)

    Simon de Chyvet 1275 V1 p117

Clay

"One who lives on the clay" or perhaps "one who works in a clay pit." (Reaney s.n. Clay)

    Roger del Clay 1350 V6 p8

Clayrod

"Of the clay clearing." The modern spelling would be Clay Royd. (Smith vii.170, 236)

    John del Clayrod 1350 V6 p5

Clerk⁺
Originally this name referred to a cleric. Eventually it came to mean a scholar, secretary, etc. Reaney mentions that it was "particularly common for one who had taken only minor orders." The modern spelling tends to be Clark or Clarke. (Reaney s.n. Clark)
    Willelmus clericus de Dewesbir(y)
    Willelmus clericus de Dewesbyry 1274 V1 p87, 88, 99

Clif
One who dwells by a slope or bank; there are some Yorkshire places modernly named Cliff or variants thereof. (Reaney s.n. Cliff, Smith viii.37-38)
    Adam del Clif 1274 V1 p98
    Alecok, Alkoc del Clif 1274 V1 p80, 111
    John del Clif 1275 V1 p134
    Lance del Clyf 1275 V1 p132
    Nicholas del Clif 1275 V1 p119
    Richard del Clif 1275 v1 p102
    Henry del Cliff 1350 V6 p2
    Robert del Cliff 1350 V6 p9, 80
    Thomas del Cliff 1351 V6 p43
    William del Clif, Cliff 1352 V6 p69, 105

Clifton
Modern Clifton. "Farmstead on the steep bank," from OE *clif* + *tūn*. (Reaney s.n. Clifton, Smith iii.3)
    Richard de Clifton 1274 V1 p83
    Michael de Cliftones 1275 V1 p152

Cokcroft
From Cockcroft, near Rishworth. Basically, a "chicken enclosure." (Smith iii.73)

John de Cokcroft 1351 V6 p55
Richard de Cokcroft 1351 V6 p55

Coldlay
Modern Coley. The name means "cold, bleak clearing," from OE *cald* + *lēah*. See also Colley, below. (Smith iii.83)
Margery de Coldlay (f) 1352 V6 p89

Coldwell
From one of several Coldwells or Cold Wells in the West Riding. The name means (as you might guess) "cold spring," from OE *cald* + *wella*. (Smith vii.167, 266)
Matilda de, del Coldwell (f) 1351 V6 p20
Thomas del Coldwell 1351 V6 p47
Richard de, del Coldwell 1352 V6 p85, 96, 105

Colley
Modern Coley. The name means "cold, bleak clearing," from OE *cald* + *lēah*. This name could be a nickname for one who is dark ("coaly") but the *de* indicates It is most likely a locative name for the place mentioned by Smith. (Smith iii.83, Reaney s.n. Colley)
Ralph de Colley 1275 V1 p137

Colpon
ME *culpoun*, a piece, a slice. Probably a name referring, as Redmonds says, to "a new piece of land cut out from the waste," so perhaps a locative reference, though possibly a nickname referring to another sort of slice. (Redmonds, *English Surnames* 20; MED s.v. culpoun; note the MED's 1385 citation from Chaucer: "*He... leet anoon comaunde to hakke and hewe / The okes olde and leyen hem on a rewe / In colpons [vr. culpouns] wel arrayed for to brenne.*")

John Colpon 1350 V6 p2
Thomas Culpon 1350 V6 p4

Connale
I do not know the source of this name. Possibly it may be from Cownall, a place now lost. Smith's cited spellings include *Counalein* in 1337. The *Conn-* spelling doesn't seem to match this but it could possibly be a misreading of *n* for *u*. *-al, -ale* is from OE *halh*, "nook or corner of land" (Smith vii.199, iii.110). Alternatively, the *conn-* element could perhaps refer to quinces (MED s.vv. quince, connates).

Thomas de Connhal 1275 V1 p117
Adam de Connhale 1275 V1 p117
William de Connhale, Connal 1275 V1 p109, 136
John de Connale 1351 V6 p40

Coplay
Modern Copley, a place with a name meaning "clearing by the hilltop" from OE *copp* + *lēah*, the headland above the river Calder. (Smith iii.110)

Thomas de Coppeley 1274 V1 p85, 86, 90, 110
Richard de Coppeley, Coppele 1274 V1 p81, 110
Henry de Coppeley, Coppley 1274 V1 p81, 124
Henry de Coplay 1350 V6 p2
Hugh de Coplay 1350 V6 p4
William de Coplay 1350 V6 p4
John de Copplay 1350 V6 p8
William de Copplay 1350 V6 p8
Matilda de Coplay (f) 1352 V6 p89

Coventre
From the name of a place in Yorkshire now lost, Coventry or Coventree. There is also a Coventry in Warwickshire but

It is not as likely to be the source here. (Smith iii.146, Reaney s.n. Coventry)
    Adam de Coventre, Coventry 1350 V6 p12, 74

Craven
From the district of Craven, which probably comes from the Welsh *craf*, "garlic." (Ekwall ODEPN s.n. Craven)
    William de Craven 1352 V6 p105

Crigeliston
Modern Crigglestone. OE *crȳc* + *hyll*; the first part is from Primitive Welsh *crüg*, meaning "a hill," the second is OE *hyll* as a tautological explanation for a Welsh word the English didn't understand. The last element is from OE *tūn*, or farmstead. (Smith ii.101, Watts s.nn. Crigglestone, Crichel)
    Pagan de Crigeliston 1274, 1275 V1 p86, 102
    Henry de Crigeliston, Crikeliston 1274 V1 p83, 100
    Alan de Crikeliston 1275 v1 p102
    Bate de Crikeliston 1275 V1 p106

Croft
"One who lives by a croft." A croft is a small piece of agricultural ground, or sometimes an enclosure or courtyard. (Reaney s.n. Croft, MED s.v. croft (n.))
    Adam del Croftes 1274 V1 p96
    William del Croft 1352 V6 p79, 87

Crosland
Modern South Crosland, "tract of land with a cross," from OE *cros* + *land*. (Smith ii.265)
    Ranulf de Crosland 1274 V1 p101
    Maude de Crosland (f) 1275 V1 p137

Cross⁺
"Dweller by a cross." (Reaney s.n. Cross)
>Adam ad Crucem 1274 V1 p93

Cumberworth
Modern Lower and Upper Cumberworth, meaning "Cumbra's enclosure," from *Cumbra* + *worð*. Cumbra is an OE personal name, ultimately from PrWelsh *Cumbroʒ, "the Welshman." (Smith ii.216)
>Hugh de Cumberworth 1275 V1 p147
>Richard de Cumbrewrth 1275 V1 p147

Cunigberg
Modern Conisbrough, "the king's fortification," from ON *konungr* (possibly replacing an earlier OE cyning) + OE *burh*. (Smith i.125, Ekwall ODEPN s.n. Conisbrough, Mills s.n. Conisbrough.)
>John de Cunigberg 1274 V1 p91

Dacreland
Dacre is a village in North Yorkshire. It is a British river name meaning "trickling stream," and the name of a river in Cumbria. In the case of the Yorkshire Dacre, the village is named after the former name of a nearby stream. However, see also Acreland. The formation *d'[placename]* is not normally seen in these records, but given the existence of a nearby Acreland, may be a possibility here. (Ekwall ODEPN s.n. Dacre, Mills s.n. Dacre)
>Jordan Dacreland 1350 V6 p5

Dalton
Modern Dalton, from OE *dæl* + *tūn*, meaning "valley town." (Smith ii.223, Reaney s.n. Dalton)

Adam de Dalton 1275 V1 p112
Henry de Dalton 1275 V1 p112

Damme
"One dwelling by the dam"; from OE *damm*. There are several places in the West Riding with "dam" as a name element. (MED s.v. dam (n.), Reaney s.n. Dams)
Alan del Damme 1351 V6 p36
Margaret del Damme, Dame (f) 1351 V6 p46, 105

Danford
I do not see a West Riding place of this name. But, per Ekwall, this is possibly "a ford in a valley," from OE *denu* + *ford*, or "the Danes' ford." (Ekwall ODEPN s.n. Denford, Danthorp, Danby)
Thomas de Danford 1350 V6 p2

Denby
From one of the Yorkshire places called Denby, probably meaning "farmstead of the Danes" from OE *Dene* + ON *bȳ*. (Smith i.326, ii.234; Mills s.n. Denby, Ekwall ODEPN s.n. Denby)
John de Denby 1350 V6 p2
Margery de Deneby (f) 1351 V6 p17

Dene
Modernly spelled "Dean" or "-den," this is a very common place name element in the West Riding. It is from OE *denu*, meaning "valley." In this context, it means "dweller in a valley." (Smith vii.178, Reaney s.n. Dean)
Jordan del Dene 1274 V1 p81
Richard del Dene 1274 V1 p94
John del Dene 1350 V6 p3

Margery del Dene (f) 1350 V6 p4
Robert del Dene 1350 V6 p16
William del Dene 1350 V6 p2
Richard del Dene 1351 V6 p15, 17, 47
Adam del Dene 1352 V6 p97

Denton
Modern Denton. A very common place name, from the OE *denu* + *tūn*, "farmstead or village in a valley." (Smith v.63, Mills s.n. Denton, Ekwall ODEPN s.n. Denton)
William de Denton 1274 V1 p98
Alan de Denton 1275 V1 p106

Dewysbiry
Modern Dewsbury. The name is "Dewi's fortification," with Old Welsh *Dewi* + OE *burh*. (Smith ii.184-185)
John de Dewysbiry 1275 V1 p127
Margery de Dewysbiry, Dewisbyry (f) 1275 V1 p118

Donecastre
From Doncaster, "fortification on the Don," the old Roman fort of Danum with OE *ceaster* (walled fort) added. The fort was on a river called Don. (Ekwall ODEPN s.n. Don, Mills s.n. Doncaster, Smith i.29)
Raymond de Donecastre 1274 V1 p90
Robert de Donecastre 1275 V1 p108

Dounom
Modern Downholme, in the North Riding. "(Settlement) at the hills," from the dative plural of OE *dūn*. (Watts s.n. Downholme)
William de Dounom 1350 V6 p11, 66 Also William Dounom

William de Downon 1352 V6 p104 Probably the same as William de Dounom

Dranefeld
OE *drān* + *feld*, "drone's field." This place was known from the 12th - 17th centuries, and modern Dransfield Hill probably takes its name from it. (Smith ii.199)
    Thomas de Dranefeld 1275 V1 p134

Dricker
Probably modern Dirtcar or Dirk Carr, "dirt marsh," from OE *drit* + ON *kjarr*, but also possibly a place name meaning "dry marsh," from OE *drȳge* + ON *kjarr*. Smith cites *Drykerrode* to 1323 and *the Drycarr* to 1766. (Smith ii.102; iii.100, 134; vii.215)
    Matthew de Dricker 1350 V6 p11

Dykman
"One who lives near or works on a ditch or dyke." From OE *dīc* + *mann*.(Reaney sn Dickman)
    Richard Dykman 1350 V6 p2

Ecclesley
Modern Exley.The origin is *eclēsia*, a British word indicating a pre-English church, along with OE *lēah*, clearing.(Smith iii.92, vii.182)
    William de Ecclesley, Ecclesey, Ecclisley, Eclisley 1274 V1 p82, 83, 114, 122, 123, 153

Eland
Modern Elland. From OE *ēa* + *land*, "land by the river." It is located on the banks of the River Calder. (Smith iii.43)
    John de Eland, Elaunde, Heland, Elaund 1274 V1 p82, 126, 108, 135, 145, 150

Eldwardholes
A medieval field name from the Fulstone area. "Æþelweald's or Ælfweard's hollow," from an OE personal name *Æþelweald* or *Ælfweard* + *hol*. Compare modern Ediholes in Lancashire, from the OE feminine personal name *Eadgeofu* + *hol*; its thirteenth and fourteenth century forms are relatively similar to these, including *Ediholes*, *Edyasholes*, *Edieles*, *Edyefholes*. (Smith ii.242; Ekwall *Lancashire* 73)

> John de Elwardeholes, Heldwardholes, Eldwardholes 1274, 1275 V1 p97, 118, 148 (Edwardeholes in the translation seems to be a typo from Elwardeholes in the Latin.)
> Adam de Eldwardholes 1275 V1 p118
> John de Elwoldehuls, Elwaldhuls, Eldwaldhuls 1350 V6 p2, 59, 88
> Agnes de Elwaldhules (f) 1352 V6 p96

Elfletburgh
Modern Elphaborough Hall. Smith suggests that the first part of the name is from an old stream name, Elflet, with the meaning "eel stream" from OE *æl* + *flēot*. (Smith iii.160)

> Adam de Elfletburgh 1351 V6 p25

Emeley
Modern Emley. "Eama's (or Emma's) forest clearing," from the OE personal name *Ēama* or **Emma* + *lēah* "clearing." (Ekwall ODEPN s.n. Emley, Smith ii.218, Watts s.n. Emley)

> Henry de Emeley, Almeley, Ammeley, Emmeley 1275 V1 p117, 137, 141, 146

Erdeslawe
Modern Ardsley. "Erd's mound," probably from OE *Eard* or *Eorēd* + *hlāw*. (Smith ii.174)
    Thomas de Erdeslawe, Erdeslew 1275 V1 p107, 126

Ernschagh
Modern Earnshaw, meaning "eagle wood." From OE *earn* + *sceaga*. (Smith i.234, Reaney s.n. Earnshaw)
    Adam de Ernschagh, Erneschagh 1351, 1352 V6 p46, 105

Estwode
Modern Eastwood, from OE *ēast* + *wudu*. (Smith i.188)
    Richard de Estwode 1275 V1 p142

Everingham
Modern Everingham, a place in the East Riding of Yorkshire. (Reaney s.n. Everingham)
    Adam de Everingham, Heveringham 1274 V1 p101, 141

Ewod
Probably modern Ewood, though the earliest version Smith mentions is 1548; From OE *īw* + *wudu*, "yew wood." (Smith iii.160)
    Matilda de Ewod (f) 1352 V6 p92

Fetherstan
Modern Featherstone, probably from OE *feoðer-* + *stān*, meaning "four stones," possibly referring to a nearby cromlech or tetralith. (Smith ii.86)
    William de F[ether]stan, Phetherstan 1275 V1 p143, 154

Farneley
Modern Farnley or Fearnley, "Woodland glade or clearing overgrown with fern," from OE *fearn* + *lēah*. There are several places of this name in the West Riding. (Smith iii.211, 33)
    Alexander de Farneley 1275 V1 p147

Fekesby
Modern fixby: "Fech's farmstead." A personal name from the OIr personal name *fiach*, *fiacc*, + ON *bȳ*. (Smith iii.35)
    Hugh de Fekesby 1274 V1 p85
    Thomas de Fekesby 1274 V1 p85
    Alan de Fekesby 1275 V1 p112

Feld
"Of the field or open country"; ME *fēld* is descended from OE *feld*. (Smith vii.185, MED s.v. fēld, Reaney sn. field)
    Thomas del Feld 1351 V6 p22
    Richard del Feld 1352 V6 p92

Fenton
Modern Church Fenton in North Yorkshire. "Enclosure by a fen," from OE *fenn* + *tūn*. (Watts s.n. Fenton)
    Thomas de Fenton 1274 V1 p82

Fery
Modern Ferrybridge, which was frequently *Feri*, *Fery*, *Feri*, etc. during the thirteenth century. Smith says "The ferry, which carried the traffic of the Great North Road across the Aire, was replaced by a bridge at the end of the twelfth century." (Smith ii.66, Reaney s.n. Ferry, MED s.v. feri(e.(n. 2))
    William de Fery 1350 V6 p11
    John de Feri de Horbure, Fery 1351 V6 p25, 29

John atte Fery 1351 V6 p31 (The *atte* may indicate that this person worked at a ferry rather than lived at Ferrybridge.)

Flanshowe
Modern Flanshaw. Probably from a personal name *Flan* + ON *haugr*: "Flan's mound or hill." Now that this meaning is forgotten, the hill there is called "Flanshaw Hill." (Smith ii.167).
　　Walter de Flanshowe 1274 V1 p86

Floketon
Modern Flockton, from the ON personal name *Flóki* and OE *tūn*, meaning "Flóki's farmstead." (Smith ii.203)
　　Michael de Floketon 1275 V1 p127
　　Edmund de Flokton 1351 V6 p50

Foldes
OE *fald* means "a fold, an enclosure" and is an element in quite a few Yorkshire names. It is not clear which particular one may be meant here. (Smith vii.184)
　　Roger del Foldes 1275 V1 p144
　　Hugh del Foldis 1275 V1 p117

Fouleston
Modern Fulstone; "Fugol's farm," OE personal name *Fugol* + *tūn*. (Smith ii.239)
　　Adam de Fugeliston 1274 V1 p97
　　John de Fugeliston 1274 V1 p97
　　Thomas de Fugeliston 1274 V1 p97
　　Annabel de Fouleston (f) 1275 V1 p146, 154
　　John de Fouleston 1275 V1 p118, 120
　　Michael de Fouleston 1275 V1 p148
　　Sarah de Fouleston (f) 1275 V1 p129

William de Fouleston 1275 V1 p119
Michael de Fuleston 1275 V1 p147
Thomas de Foughelston 1351 V6 p17, 58

Fresley
Probably modern Freasley, in Polesworth, Warwickshire, which is about 90 miles away from Wakefield. I could not find a Yorkshire name that would have been spelled this way; there is a Farsley listed in Smith and in Watts but there is no evidence for a *Fr-* spelling. It is not a common surname in the Rolls, so it is not impossible that it is a name from outside Yorkshire. The Fresley spelling has been used for the Warwickshire location. (Denholm-Young 116)

Philip de Fresley, Frechley 1275 V1 p113, 114

Friston
Modern Ferry Fryston, probably from an OE *Frīstun*, from *Frīsa* + *tūn*, farm of the Frisians. (Smith ii.65)

William de Friston 1352 V6 p77 chaplain

Frith
Frith in ME meant a park, a woodland meadow, or a wilderness, as well as a royal forest. So this name means, essentially, "of the woods." From OE *fyrhþ(e)*, wood, woodland. (Smith vii.190, MED s.v. frith (n. 2))

Alcok de, del Fryth, Frith 1274 V1 p96, 147
Walter del Fritht 1275 V1 p140
John del Frith 1350 V6 p7

Fyney
Modern Fenay; Smith says this is probably a compound of OE and ON *finn* "coarse grass," and OE *ēg* "land partly surrounded by water." (Smith ii.258, Reaney s.n. finney)
    John del Fyney 1274 V1 p83

Gledehul
Modern Gledhill, meaning "kite hill," from OE *gleoda* + *hyll*.(Reaney s.n. Gledhill, Smith ii.258)
    William del Gledehul 1275 V1 p112

Godeby
From Goadby or Goadby Marwood in Leicestershire. The name elements are the personal name *Gouti* + ON *bȳ*, so this was "Gouti's farm or village." (Reaney s.n. Goadby, Ekwall ODEPN s.n. Goadby, Smith vii.195)
    Henry de Godeby 1274 V1 p99

Godlay
Either modern Godly or the place now lost called Godley, meaning either "good clearing" or "Goda's clearing," from OE *gōd* + *lēah*. (Smith iii.72, 98). In the case of Henry Godley, this may also be a nickname for one that is noble, valiant, or virtuous. (MED s.v. gōdlī (adj. (2)))
    Henry Godley 1275 v1 p104 (this is possibly a
        nickname, not a locative name)
    John de Godlay, Godley 1350 V6 p4, 10
    William de Godlay 1350 V6 p2
    Johanna de Godlay (f) 1352 V6 p104

Goldeley
I cannot find a modern place name to which this is connected. It would most likely be spelled "Goldley." Possibly an OE personal name such as *Golda* + *lēah*,

meaning "Golda's clearing." (Smith s.n. Gold, Watts s.n. Goldthorpe)
>   Adam de Goldeley 1275 V1 p111
>   Alice de Goldeley (f) 1275 V1 p128

Goldhore
Possibly a name descended from OE *golde* + *ōra*, "place where marigolds grow." ME *hōr* means "gray or white" but I do not see any evidence of it in a compound with gold. (Reaney s.n. Golder, MED hōr)
>   Nigel Goldhore 1351 V6 p49

Goukethorp
Modern Gawthorpe, meaning "cuckoo settlement"; from ON *gaukr* + ON, ODan *þorp*. Ekwall suggests that *Gaukr* was also a personal name with the same origin, so it could be "Gaukr's settlement," and Smith and Watts add that the ON *gaukr* was also a name for a simpleton or fool, so these name might also mean "fool's settlement." There are several places of this name in the West Riding. (Ekwall ODEPN s.n. Gawthorp; Smith ii.102, 230; Watts s.nn. Gawthorpe Hall, Gawthrop)
>   Henry de Goukethorpe 1274 V1 p83
>   Hanne de Goukethorp 1275 V1 p108
>   Robert de Goukethorpe 1275 V1 p129

Grayne
"One who lives at an inlet or fork of a river," from ON *grein*. (Reaney s.n. Grain, MED s.v. grein)
>   John Grayne 1352 V6 p75

Grene
"One who lives by the village green." (Reaney s.n. Green, MED s.v. grēne (n.(1)))

Elias del Grene, Gren 1274 V1 p80, 112
Richard del Grene 1274 V1 p98
Henry del Grene 1275 V1 p118
Thomas del Grene 1275 V1 p117
William del Grene of Ossete 1275 V1 p109
Edmund del Grene 1350 V6 p7
Richard del Grene 1350 V6 p2
William del Grene 1350 V6 p2, 13, 48
Adam del Grene 1351 V6 p29, 58
John del Grene 1351 V6 p17
Margery del Grene (f) 1351 V6 p23
Robert del Grene 1351 V6 p23
Agnes del Grene (f) 1352 V6 p98
Henry del Grene of Criglestone 1352 V6 p109

Grenhill
"One who lives by a green hill, or by a place named Green Hill"; there are several small places by this name in the West Riding. From OE *grēne* + *hyll*. (Reaney s.n. Greenhill, Smith vii.211)
Thomas del Grenhill 1350 V6 p15

Grenhirst
Modern Greenhurst Hey, or a more general reference to "one who lives by the green wooded-hill." From OE *grēne* + *hyrst*. (Reaney s.n. Greenist, Smith iii.175)
John de, del Grenehirst, Grenhirst 1274 V1 p93, 116
Robert del Grenhirst 1275 V1 p152
Nicholas del Grenhirst 1352 V6 p71

Grenwode
Modern High Greenwood, or in some cases (such as that of John del Grenwode) this may just mean "one who lives by

a green wood." From OE *grēne* + *wudu*. (Smith iii.191, Reaney s.n. Greenwood)
    John del Grenwode 1275 V1 p126
    Johanna de Grenwod (f) 1351 V6 p42

Gretton
Reaney suggests this is from the places called either Girton (Cambs, Notts) or Gretton (Glos, Northants). Noting also the presence in these records of Robert de Grotton, this may be an error for the Yorkshire place Grotton, with a name originating possibly from OE *grota* "particle of sand" or *groten* "gravelly, sandy" + *tūn*. (Smith ii.319, Reaney s.n Girton)
    William de Gretton 1275 v1 p104

Grimeston
Modern Grimston, "Grimr's farmstead," from the OScand personal name *Grímr* + OE *tūn*. There are quite a few Grimstons in Yorkshire and elsewhere. (Smith vii.294, Ekwall ODEPN s.n. Grimston, Reaney s.n. Grimston, Mills s.n. Grimston)
    Alan de Grimeston 1275 V1 p129

Grotton
Modern Grotton, with a name originating possibly from OE *grota* "particle of sand" or *groten* "gravelly, sandy" + *tūn*. See also Gretton. (Smith ii.319)
    Robert de Grotton 1352 V6 p106

Habbas
I cannot find the source of this name.
    Agnes de Habbas (f) 1351 V6 p46

Hage
Modern Haigh, from OE *haga*, "enclosure." (Smith vii.199)
>John del Hage 1351 V6 p48

Haldewrth
Modern Holdsworth. The meaning is "Halda's enclosure" from OE personal name *Halda* + *worþ*. (Smith iii.114)
>John de Haldewrth 1275 V1 p110
>William de Haldwrth 1350 V6 p8
>John Haldwrth senior 1352 V6 p69
>Otes de Haldwrth 1352 V6 p100
>Richard de Haldwrth 1352 V6 p72

Halghton
Modern Halton, in the West Riding near Leeds, though there are several other Haltons including ones in Lancashire and North Yorkshire that could also be a source for this name. The name means "a farmstead in a nook or corner of land," from OE *halh* + *tūn*. (Mills s.n. Halton, Ekwall ODEPN s.n. Halton.)
>William de Halghton 1350 V6 p12

Halifax
Modern Halifax, a large city in West Yorkshire. The origin of the place name is uncertain; the theory mentioned in both Smith and Mills is that it means something like "a place with coarse grass in a nook or corner of land," from OE *halh* + **gefeaxe*. (Smith iii.104, Mills s.n. Halifax)
>Henry de Halifax 1274 V1 p80
>Bate de Halifax 1275 V1 p111
>John de Halifax 1275 V1 p125
>William de Halifax 1275 V1 p125
>John de Halyfax 1350 V6 p11, 91
>Thomas de Halyfax 1350 V6 p16

Halle

Aula is Latin for "hall; church/temple; palace/castle; inner/royal court; courtiers; royal power." "Hall" is the likely meaning for *Aula* here, and the name probably refers to a servant at the hall. The English vernacular version of the name is probably *del Halle*, which is seen in the fourteenth century records, or *de la Sale*, "of the hall," from OE *sæl*. (Reaney s.nn. Sale, Sall)

    Adam de Aula de Sandal 1274 V1 p91
    Thomas de Aula 1275 V1 p142
    Thomas del Hall 1351 V6 p42
    James del Halle 1350 V6 p1
    James del Halle of Sandale 1351 V6 p26
    John del Halle, Hall 1351 V6 p24, 44

Halumschyre

Modern Hallam, from one of two proposed origins: "(place at) the rocks," from OScand *hallr* or OE *hall* in a dative plural form, *hallum*; or "(place at) the nooks or corners of land," from OE *halh* in the dative plural form *halum*. (Mills s.n. Hallam, Ekwall ODEPN s.n. Hallam)

    Thomas de Halumschyre of Bradeford, Halumschyre
        1275 V1 p142, 149

Harrop

There are several "Harrop" place names in the West Riding, with the meaning "hare valley." From OE *hara* + *hop*. (Smith iii.275, Reaney s.n. Harrop)

    Robert de Harrop, Harop 1274 V1 p98, 149

Hartisheved

Modern Hartshead, meaning "the hart's head," from OE *heorot* + *hēafod*. (Smith iii.6)

    Matilda de Hartisheved (f) 1350 V6 p7

Haycroft
One who "dwells by the hay-croft." From OE *hēg* + *croft*.
(Reaney s.nn. Haycraft, Croft; MED s.vv. hei, croft)
> Nicholas del Haycroft 1352 V6 p90

Haylay
One who dwells "at a hay clearing." From OE *hēg* + *lēah*.
Smith mentions a place in the West Riding named Hayley, but does not include a medieval citation. See also Helay.
(Reaney s.n. Hailey, Smith iii.264)
> John de Haylay 1351 V6 p55

Heckeshill
Modern Eccleshill, from Brit *eclēsia* "church" + OE *hyll*.
(Smith iii.258-9).
> Richard de Heckeshill 1275 V1 p129

Hecmundewyk
Modern Heckmondwike, from OE personal name *Hēahmund* + *wīc*, "dairy farm." (Smith iii.24)
> John de Hecmundewyk 1275 V1 p132

Hedon
Modern Hedon. "Heath hill," from OE *hæth* + *dūn*. Possibly also "a hill or down where hay is made," from OE *hēg* + *dūn*. See also Heton, Heydon. (Mills s.n. Haydon, Reaney s.n. Hayden, Watts s.n. Hedon)
> Richard de Hedon 1275 V1 p149

Heydon
I do not see a Yorkshire place with this name, but there are several others. The name generally means "a hill or down where hay is made," from OE *hēg* + *dūn*. See also Hedon,

Heton. (Mills s.n. Haydon, Reaney s.n. Hayden.)
   Richard de Heydon 1274 V1 p81

Hegh
Possibly "of the high"; meaning high ground, or perhaps an individual's height. (MED s.v. heigh). There are several place names in the West Riding that might be referred to here as well. (See also Hage.)
   Thomas del Hegh 1351 V6 p67

Hegrode
"Enclosed clearing," from OE *(ge)hæg + rod*. Possibly Heyrod in Lancashire. (Smith vii.198, 236, Ekwall *Lancashire* 29.)
   William de Hegrode 1275 V1 p139
   Adam de Heyrod, Herod 1352 V6 p75, 79

Helbroke
Perhaps modern Holbrook in Derbyshire, about 60 miles from Wakefield. "Brook in a hollow," from OE *hol + broc*. (Watts s.n. Holbrook)
   Henry de Helbroke 1275 V1 p131

Heley
From one of several places modernly spelled Healey or Healaugh. The meaning is "high clearing," from OE *hēah + lēah*. (Smith ii.180, 188, 249, 212; Watts s.n. Healey)
   Adam de Heley, Helye, Heleys, Helay 1275 V1 p87,
      91, 120, 121
   Alot de Heley (f) 1275 V1 p119
   William de Heley 1275 V1 p141 same as William son
      of Adam de Heley?
   Roger de Heyleye, Heleyes 1275 V1 p104, 145

Helgate

Possibly modern "Hall Gate," or "Hallgate"; -*gate* meant a road or street, from ON *gata*. See also Holgate. (MED s.v. gāte n. (2))

    Henry de Helgate 1275 V1 p136

Helgrene

Possibly a modern "Hillgreen." I have not found this place name.

    Hugh del Helgrene 1275 V1 p106

Helistones

Modern Ellistones. Smith suggests the origin is from OE *hǣlig* + *stān*, meaning "unstable stones." (Smith iii.47)

    John de Helistones 1274 V1 p80
    Michael de Helistones, Helyston, Elistones,
        Helystones 1274 V1 p80, 126, 136, 138

Helm

"Of the cattle shelter," so this locative name implies an occupational purpose as a name for a herdsman. OE *helm*, meaning "a covering," later meant "a roofed cattle shelter." (Reaney s.n. Helm)

    Roger del Helm 1275 V1 p151
    William del Helm 1275 V1 p152

Helyleigh

Perhaps modern High Lee. -*leigh* is, of course, "clearing in a wood" from OE *lēah*. This name could be a "hillock clearing" with OE *hygel* or a "high clearing" with OE *hēah*. (Smith iii.137)

    Thomas del, de Helyleigh, Haylyleght, Hylyleigh,
        Hylileigh, Heyliligh, Heylyligh, Hylyligh, Hylilegh
        1350, 1351 V6 p5, 23, 55, 72, 73, 74, 85

Hengandrod

From one of several place names in West Yorkshire now called Hanging Royd. The meaning is "steep-sloping clearing," from OE *hangende* "hanging, steep" + *rod* "clearing." (Smith iii.87, 160, 189; vii.201, 236.)

    Adam del Hengandrod 1351 V6 p23
    John del Hengandrod 1351 V6 p55
    Alexander del Hengenrod 1351 V6 p42

Heppewrth

Modern Hepworth. Smith suggests this name is from an unrecorded OE personal name *Heppa* + OE *worð*, "enclosure," so "Heppa's enclosure." (Smith ii.242, Mills s.n. Hepworth)

    Adam de Heppewrth 1274 V1 p82, 98
    Henry de Heppewrth 1274 V1 p98
    Jordan de Heppewrth 1274 V1 p98
    Simon de Heppewrth 1274 V1 p98 "de eadem"
    Thomas de Heppewrth, Eppewrth 1274 V1 p88, 109
    Warin de Heppewrth 1275 V1 p118
    Juliana de Hepwrth (f) 1351 V6 p47
    Richard de Heppwrth 1351 V6 p18
    William de Hepwrth 1351 V6 p18

Heptonstall

Modern Heptonstall. A "hip or dog-rose farmstead" from OE *hēope* "hip, fruit of the wild rose" or *hēopa* "dog-rose, bramble" + *tūn-stall* "farmstead." (Smith iii.191).

    Nalke de Heptonstall 1274 V1 p94

Heth

"One who dwells on the heath," from OE *hæð*. (Reaney s.n. Heath)

    Robert del Heth 1351 V6 p20

Heton

Modern Heaton. From OE *hēah* + *tūn*, "high farmstead." This is a relatively common place name. (Smith iii.245, Mills s.n. Heaton) See also Hedon.

    John de Heton 1274 V1 p89, 101
    Adam de Heton 1275 V1 p142
    Henry de Heton 1275 V1 p142
    Hugh de Heton 1275 V1 p69
    Robert de Heton 1275 V1 p147
    William de Heton 1275 V1 p147
    John de Heton 1351 V6 p37

Heves

Probably "of the hives," perhaps a beekeeper. (MED s.v. hīve (n.))

    William del Heves 1352 V6 p78

Hey

"One who dwells by the enclosure," from OE *(ge)hæg*. (Reaney s.n. Hay)

    Richard del Hey 1352 V6 p68

Hill

"One who dwells on the hill" from OE *hyll*. (Reaney s.n. Hill)

    Henry del Hill 1351 V6 p44
    John del Hille 1352 V6 p89

Hilton

Hilton is in the North Riding, and there are Hiltons in other counties as well. The meaning is "hilltop enclosure, farmstead, or village," from OE *hyll* + *tūn*. (Reaney s.n. Hilton, Smith vii.211, 257)

    John de Hilton 1351 V6 p20

Hiperom

Modern Hipperholme, meaning "amongst the osiers," from OE *hyper*, "osier" + *-um*, the dative plural ending. (Smith iii.79; vii.212, 262)

    Alice, Alote de Hyperum (f) 1275 V1 p116, 129
    Peter de Hyperum 1275 V1 p144
    Richard de Hyperum 1275 V1 p112
    Roger de Hyperum 1275 V1 p110
    Adam de Hiperom 1350 V6 p5
    Annabel de Hiperom (f) 1350 V6 p8
    Thomas de Hiperom 1350 V6 p9
    William de Hiperom 1351 V6 p20
    Robert de Hiperom of Rothewell 1352 V6 p101, 104

Hirst

"One who lives in the wood or on the wooded hill," from OE *hyrst* "wood, wooded hill." (Reaney s.n. Herst)

    William del, de Hirst, Hyrst 1275 V1 p125, 126, 144

Hoglay

"Hog clearing," from OE *hogg* + *lēah*, but Smith points out that the first element could possibly be the surname *Hog*; in that case, this is "Hog's clearing." (Smith ii.263)

    Isabella de Hoglay (f) 1351 V6 p47

Holdfeld

This could be one of several modern places, including Oldfields and Lower & Upper Oldfield, or perhaps just "an old open field." From OE *ald* + *feld*. (Smith iii.262, 139)

    Richard de Holdfeld 1275 V1 p115
    Roger del Holdfeld 1351 V6 p34

Hole
"One who lives in a hollow." There are also several fields named "Hole" or "The Hole" in West Yorkshire. From OE and ON *hol*, "hollow." (Reaney s.n. Hole; Smith iii.152, 251, ii.104)

    Richard del Hole 1350 V6 p8
    Thomas del Hole 1350 V6 p2
    Alice del Hole (f) 1351 V6 p17
    William del Hole 1351 V6 p33
    Henry del Hole 1352 V6 p99

Holebroke
Perhaps modern Holbrook in Derbyshire, about 60 miles from Wakefield, or another place that is a "brook in a hollow." "One who lives by the brook in the hollow," from OE *hol*, ON *holr* "hollow, sunken, lying in a hollow" + OE *brōc*. See also Helbroke. (Watts s.n. Holbrook)

    Henry de Holebroke 1274 V1 p86

Holgate
Modern Holgate, or "one who lives by the road in the hollow," from OE *hol*, ON *holr* "hollow" + ON *gata* "road, cattle walk, or pasture." See also Helgate. (Reaney s.n. Holgate, Smith vii.192, 206)

    Thomas de Holgate 1274 V1 p93 94
    Henry de Holgate 1275 V1 p152
    John de Holgate 1275 V1 p125
    Cecelia, Cecilia de Holgate (f) 1350 V6 p5, 43
    Henry de Holgate 1351 V6 p22

Holirakes
Reaney says "From some small spot in the West Riding." This could be the modern place Hollin Rakes (Cowling), or the lost places listed in Smith as Hollinrake and Hollin

Dracke. The name means "rough path near the holly tree," from OE *holegn* "holly" + *hraca* "rough narrow path, cattle- or sheep-walk." (Reaney s.n. Hollingrake, Smith iii.175, 277)

    Adam del Holirakes 1275 V1 p117

Holm

Possibly from the place modernly called Holme, from OE *holegn*, "holly." However, this name may also mean "one who lives near a piece of flat land in a fen, or by land partly surrounded by streams, from ON *holmr*. The place Holme is usually spelled Holne in the 1270s Rolls, so this name may represent the latter meaning. See also Holne. (Reaney s.n. Holm, Smith ii.269)

    William del Holm 1274 V1 p94
    William del Holme 1351 V6 p59

Holne

Modern Holme, from OE *holegn*, "holly tree." However, in some cases this name may also mean "one who lives near a piece of flat land in a fen, or by land partly surrounded by streams, from ON *holmr* "water meadow." See also Holm. (Reaney s.n. Holm, Smith ii.269, vii.207)

    Benedict de Holne 1274 V1 p98, 118
    John de Holne 1274 V1 p97, 98. 149
    Matthew de Holne 1274 V1 p98
    William de Holne 1274 V1 p98, 148 (on p. 148,
        misspelled "Honle")
    Brun de Holne 1275 V1 p118
    Robert de Holne 1275 V1 p120
    Thomas de Holne 1275 V1 p149
    Thomas del, de Holme, Holne 1351 V6 p18, 64, 66
        (Thomas "del Holme" and "de Holne" appear to be
        the same man)

Holok
"One who lives by the little hollow," from OE *holoc*, a diminutive of *hol*. (Reaney s.n. Hollock)
    John de, del Holok 1352 V6 p102, 104

Holway
"One who lives by a sunken road," from OE *holh* + *weg*. (Reaney s.n. Holloway)
    John de Holway 1350 V6 p14, 60

Honeley
Modern Honley. "Woodland glade where woodcock abound, or where there are stones and rocks," from OE *hana* "cock" or *hān* "stone" + *lēah* "meadow, enclosure." (Mills s.n. Honley, Smith ii.271)
    John de Honeley 1274 V1 p90
    Gilbert de Honley 1274 V1 p97

Hoperburn
I am not sure what this place is. *-burn* probably means "waterway," from OE *burna*, but the first element might be from OE **hōpere* "cooper" or perhaps **hoppere* "dancer" (MED s.v. bōurn(e), Smith vii.207)
    Adam de Hoperburn 1351 V6 p33

Hopton
Modern Lower and Upper Hopton (Upper Hopton being the old village). "Farmstead in the side valley," from OE *hop* "enclosure in marshland, small enclosed valley" + *tūn*. (Smith ii.198)
    Thomas de Hopton, Opton 1274 V1 p85, 146

Horbiry

Modern Horbury. "Fortification on dirty, muddy land," from OE *horu* "filth, dirt" + *birh* "fortification" (dative *byrig*). (Smith ii.150; Mills s.n. Horbury; Ekwall ODEPN s.n. Horbury suggests another possible derivation, from OE *hord*, meaning "hoard, treasure"—one thirteenth C spelling in Smith has a *d*)
 John de Horbiry, Horbyry 1274 y Sir V1 p83, 144
 Adam de Horbiry, Horbure, Horbire 1350 V6 p2, 84
 Elias de Horbire, Horbiry 1350 V6 p1, 67
 John de Horbure 1350 V6 p11, 34

Horn

Possibly "one who lives near a spur or tongue of land," from *horn*, "a projecting headland." Modern Horn Hill was *Underhorne* in 1307. (Reaney s.n. Horn, Smith ii.240)
 Richard de Horn 1275 V1 p118

Horsfall

Modern Horsefall, in Todmorden. "Horse clearing," from OE *hors* "horse" + *(ge)fall* "a place where trees have been felled." (Smith iii.182, Reaney s.n. Horsfall)
 Adam del Horsfall 1352 V6 p71

Horton

Probably from modern Great Horton. The name means "dirty or muddy farmstead," from OE *horu* + *tūn*. (Smith iii.245, Mills s.n. Horton)
 John de Horton 1274 V1 p81

Houerum

Modern Northowram, Southowram, or just a name meaning "on the slopes" (Northowram and Southowram are two ridges in the area, between which runs Shibden Brook).

From OE *æt uferum*, *ufer* being a variant of *ofer*, "a slope, hill, ridge." (Smith iii.89, 96)
    Richard de Houerum 1275 V1 p110

Houwrth
Modern Haworth. "Enclosure with a hedge," from OE *haga* "hedge" + *worð* "enclosure." (Smith iii.261, Mills s.n. Haworth, Reaney s.n. Haworth)
    Roger de Houwrth 1275 V1 p128

Hoverthoung
Modern Upperthong. From OE *þwang* "a thong" which came to mean "a narrow strip of land." (Smith ii.286, 288)
    Agnes de Hoverthoung (f) 1275 V1 p142

Huclay
I am not sure which place name this is, but perhaps it means "clearing near a bend or hill-spur," from OE *hōc* + *lēah*. Hawkley in Lancashire seems unlikely. (Reaney s.n. Hook, Ekwall *Lancashire* 104)
    John de Huclay 1351 V6 p42

Hudresfeld
Modern Huddersfield. Probably "Hudrǣd's open land," from an unrecorded OE name, **Hudrǣd*, + *feld* "open country." (Smith ii.296, Mills s.n. Huddersfield)
    Roger de Hudresfeld 1274 V1 p87
    Adam de Hodresfeld 1275 V1 p118
    William de Hudresfeld 1350 V6 p16

Hyngcliff
Modern Hinchcliffe Mill, "steep cliff," from the OE compound *henge-clif*. (Reaney s.n. Hinchcliffe, Smith ii.237)

William de Hyngcliff 1351 V6 p17
Johanna de Hyngeclif (f) 1351 V6 p65
Thomas de Hyngecliff, Hyngcliff, Hynglif 1351 V6
   p17, 18, 105

Illyngwrth

Modern Illingworth. The meaning is "Illa's enclosure," from the OE personal names *Ylla* or **Illa* + *-ing* (connective particle) + *worð* "enclosure." (Reaney s.n. Illingworth, Watts s.n. Illingworth, Smith iii.114)
   John de Ilyngwrth, Ilingworth 1350 V6 p2, 92
   Matthew de Illyngwrth, Ylingword 1350 V6 p3, 8, 23
      Also just "Matthew Ilingwrth"

Irland

"From Ireland." Hibernia is the Latin name of Ireland. (Reaney s.n. Ireland, OED s.v. Hibernian).
   Ralph de Hybernia 1274 V1 p86
   Jacke de Yreland 1275 v1 p103 "stole a robe of
      burrell, trimmed with black lamb-skin, value 8s
      6d... therefore let him be hanged."
   John de Irland of Flotten 1351 V6 p29

Karleton

There are quite a few places named (modernly) Carlton or Carleton in Yorkshire. Likely possibilities for this one include Carleton in Pontefract, or Carlton near Lofthouse, which was included in the Domesday Book as *Carlentone*. The name means "churl's farmstead," from ON *karl* + OE *tūn*. Smith says this is most likely a "Scandinavian form of the common OE *ceorla-tūn*." (Smith ii.71, 137)
   Jordan de Karleton 1275 V1 p137

Kent
"From Kent." (Reaney s.n. Kent)
>Thomas de Kent 1352 V6 p91 servant

Ker
"One who lives by a marsh or fen." From ON *kjarr*, ME *kerr*. (Reaney s.n. Carr, MED s.v. kēr)
>John del Ker 1275 V1 p128
>Richard del Kerre 1351 V6 p23

Kesburgh
Modern Kexbrough. "Stronghold of a man named Keptr," from ON *Keptr* + OE *burh*. (Mills s.n. Kexbrough, Ekwall ODEPN s.n. Kexbrough)
>Margery de Kesburgh (f) 1351 V6 p17
>John de Kessburgh 1352 V6 p96

Ketilthorp
Modern Kettlethorpe Hall. "Ketill's outlying farmstead," from *Ketill* (an ON personal name) + *þorp*. (Smith ii.103)
>John de Ketelesthorp 1275 V1 p106
>Thomas de Ketilthorp 1350 V6 p2, 48
>Elizabeth de Ketilthorp (f) 1352 V6 p106
>Robert de Ketilthorp 1352 V6 p106

Kipax
Modern Kippax. "Ash tree of a man named **Cippa* or **Cyppa*." This is an OE personal name, but probably replaced by a name using the Scandinavian *K*. The second element is OE *æsc*. (Smith vii.89, Mills s.n. Kippax, Ekwall ODEPN s.n. Kippax)
>William de Kipax 1352 V6 p92

Kirk⁺
"One who lives by the church," from ON kirkja. This was probably the vernacular form of this name, but the name in the 1275 Rolls is given in Latin. The Wakefield Rolls in 1333 include Hugh del Kirk. (Reaney s.n. Kirk, Walker 224)
    Ricardus ad Ecclesiam 1275 V1 p92, 128

Kyrkeby
From one of the several Kirkbys in West Yorkshire, at least one of which is now lost. This usually means "farmstead with a church," ON *kirkju* + *by*. (Smith ii.40, 79, 219)
    John de Kirkeby, Kyrkeby 1275 V1 p117, 127
    Henry de Kyrkeby 1275 V1 p132

Lache
Reaney suggests some origins of this name might be place names in Cheshire or Gloucestershire, but in these Yorkshire names, perhaps the other origin Reaney mentions is more likely: from residence near a stream or wet place, from OE *læcc, *lecc "stream." (Reaney s.n. Latch)
    Henry de Lache 1275 V1 p111
    John de Lache 1275 V1 p111

Lane
"One who lives in the lane," from OE *lane*. (Reaney s.n. Lane, MED s.v. lāne)
    Beatrice del Lane (f) 1350 V6 p5
    Henry del Lane 1350 V6 p10, 42
    Margery del Lane (f) 1351 V6 p34
    Thomas del Lane 1351 V6 p60
    Henry del Lane the younger 1352 V6 p92

Langfeud
Modern Longfield, from OE *lang* + *feld* "long stretch of open land." (Smith iii.175)
    William de Langfeud 1274 V1 p81, 111
    John de Langefeld 1275 v1 p104
    Robert de Langefeud 1275 V1 p117
    Thomas de Langfeud, son of John (de Langefeld) 1275
        V1 p104, 105
    Henry de Langfeld 1352 V6 p79

Langlay
There were several places with this name in the West Riding. It is from OE *lang* + *lēah* "long clearing." (Smith ii.137, 258, Reaney s.n. Langley)
    Juliana de Longeley (f) 1274 V1 p101
    Hugh de Langlay 1350 V6 p4
    Richard de Langlay 1350 V6 p2
    Thomas de Langlay 1351 V6 p55

Lascy
This noble family was of Norman origin. The name comes from the place in Normandy modernly called Lassy, in Calvados. (Reaney s.n. Lacey).
    Aleysia de Lascy (f) 1275 V1 p106, 153
    Henry de Lascy 1275 V1 p113
    Henry de Lascy 1352 V6 p89

Lethe
"Of the the barn," from ON *hlaða*, referring to a barn worker. This element is part of quite a few place names in the West Riding. (Reaney s.n. Lathe, Smith vii.204)
    Adam de Lethe, Leth, Letthe, Legthe 1275 V1 p108,
        122, 144, 154

John de Lethe, Leth, Letthe 1275 V1 p108, 144, 154
John del Lathe 1350 V6 p9

Leighrod
This is probably "woods/meadow clearing," from OE *lēah* + *rod*. One modern spelling of the surname would be Learoyd. (Smith vii.219, 236, 281)
Richard de Leighrod 1350 V6 p2
Matilda del Leighrod (f) 1351 V6 p44

Letteby
Leckby, in the North Riding. ON *Liōt* or **Liōti* (personal names) + *bȳ*, so "Liōt's or Liōta's farmstead." Ekwall mentions that ON *liótr* means "ugly." (Ekwall ODEPN s.n. Leckby)
William de Letteby 1275 V1 p123

Leyton
Reaney suggests several possible origins for this, including a Layton in the North Riding. (Reaney s.n. Layton)
Henry de Leyton 1275 V1 p147

Lidgate
From one of many places of that name in Yorkshire, from OE *hlið-geat*, "swing-gate." Modern spellings include Lidgate, Lidget, Ludgate, Lydgate, and others. (Smith vii.205)
Philip Attelidgate, atte Lidgate 1274, 1275 V1 p6, 27, 78

Litelwode
One who lives by the little wood, or the West Riding place modernly named Littlewood. From OE *lytil* + *wudu*. (Reaney s.n. Littlewood, Smith ii.254)

Geoffrey de Lyttlewode, Littlewode, Litelwode 1274 V1 p97
Geppe de Litilwode, 1274 V1 p98, 120
Hugh de Litelwode, Lytelwode 1274 V1 p98, 148
John de Litelwode 1274 V1 p120
Nicholas de Litelwode 1275 V1 p118
William de Litelwode 1275 V1 p118

Lithclif
Modern Lightcliffe. The meaning is "light, bright bank" from OE *leoht* + *clif*. (Smith iii.80)
Roger de Lithclif 1275 V1 p115

Litheseles
Modern Lighthazles, meaning "the bright hazels," from OE *leoht* + *hæsel*. (Smith iii.64)
Agnes de Litheseles (f) 1274 V1 p81
Adam de Lictheseles, Litheseles 1275 V1 p109, 124
Henry de Lytheseles, Licheseles, 1275 V1 p94, 109, 150-151
Beatrix del Lyghthesels (f) 1351 V6 p42

Locwod
Modern Lockwood. "Wood near the enclosure," from OE *loc* + *wudu*. (Smith ii.275)
William de Locwod 1351 V6 p34
John de Locwode 1275 V1 p112

Loftus
Modern Lofthouse, "house with a loft or upper chamber." From ON *lopt-hús* of the same meaning. (Smith ii.136)
Robert de Lofhus 1275 V1 p128 Probably the same as Robert the son of Hugh de Loftus

Anibil de Loftus (f) 1275 V1 p47, 125
Hugh de Loftus 1275 V1 p125

Longbothom
"One who lives by the long valley-bottom." From OE *lang* + *boðm, botm*. Smith says this particular valley was a long stretch along the River Calder. (Smith iii.138, Reaney s.n. Longbottom)
    Juliana del Longbothom (f) 1352 V6 p92
    Thomas de, del Longbottom, Longbothom 1350, 1351
        V6 p3, 42

Loppisheved
Modern Lupset. The first element is questionable according to Smith; possibly it could be from an OE personal name, **Hluppa*, or instead the ME byname *Lupe* (from OFr *loup*, "wolf"). The second element, OE *heāfod*, here means "headland." (Smith ii.155, Reaney s.n. Lupsett)
    Ralph de Lopissheved 1275 V1 p131
    Richard de Lupesheved 1275 V1 p142
    Roger de Loppisheved 1275 V1 p138
    William de Lupesheved, Lopisheved, Loppesheved,
        Loppisheved 1275 V1 p106, 129, 138

Loudeham
I have not found a source location in Yorkshire, but there are Loudhams in Nottinghamshire and Suffolk. (The former is a more likely source.) (Reaney s.n. Loudham)
    Thomas de Loudeham 1275 V1 p131

Loukes
"One from Luick (Liége). (Reaney s.n. Luke)
    John de Loukes 1351 V6 p46
    William de Loukes 1350, 1351 V6 p2, 59

Mekesburgh
Modern Mexborough. "Mēoc's or Mjúkr's fort." From OE **Mēoc* or ON *Mjúkr* + OE *burh*. (Mills s.n. Mexborough, Ekwall ODEPN s.n. Mexborough)
    William de Mekesburgh 1351 V6 p20

Mere
"Of the lake," from ME *mēre*. (MED s.v. mēre (n. (2)))
    Thomas del Meire 1351 V6 p26 (While there are several possibilities for this name, given the use of *del* and the existence of the byname *del Mere* in *Isabella del Mere*, I think this is most likely another form of *Mere*.)
    Isabella del Mere (f) 1352 V6 p93

Mersshe
"Of the marsh, one who lives by the marsh." From OE *mersc*, *merisc*. (Reaney s.n. March, MED s.v. mersh (n.))
    Thomas del Mersshe 1352 V6 p97

Metheley
Modern Methley. The origin is unsure, but might be "clearing with mown grass," from OE *mǣð* "mowing, mowing grass" + OE *lēah*, or "middle land between rivers" from ON *meðal* "middle" + OE *ēg* "island, land partly surrounded by water." The location is marshy so the latter seems more likely. (Smith ii.125, Mills s.n. Methley)
    Henry de Metheley 1274 V1 p93
    Peter de Metheley 1275 V1 p140

Miggeley
Modern Midgley. "Midge-infested clearing" or "Clearing with a manure heap," from OE *mycg* "midge" or *micge* "urine" + *lēah*. (Smith iii.132)

John de Miggeley, Migeley, Miggele 1274 V1 p80, 88, 89, 94, 117
Adam de Miggele 1275 V1 p116
Robert de Miggle 1275 V1 p147
Thomas de Myglay 1350 V6 p12
Margery de Miggelay (f) 1351 V6 p43
John de Miggeley 1352 V6 p93

Milne
"One who lives or works at the mill." OE *mylen*. (Reaney s.n. Miln)
Adam del Milne 1351 V6 p55
Margery del Milne (f) 1352 V6 p105

Milnthorp
Modern Milnthorpe. "Outlying farmstead with a mill," from ON *myln* + *þorp*.
Thomas de Milnthorp 1352 V6 p76

Mire
"One who lives by a marsh," from ON *mýrr*. (Reaney s.n. Myer, MED s.v. mīre (n. (1)))
Hugo del Mire 1274 V1 p96

Mixenden
Modern Mixenden. "Dung-heap valley," from OE *mixen* + *denu*. (Smith iii.115)
Henry de Mixenden 1274 V1 p85 89

Monte
"One who lives on the mountain or hill." There are several place names in the area modernly called Mount or The Mount. From OE *munt*, AFr *mount*. (Smith vii.225, MED

s.v. mŏunt (n. (1)))
    Adam de Monte 1275 V1 p132

More
"One who lives in or near a moor," from OE mōr "moor, marsh, fen." There are many places in Yorkshire for which this name would be appropriate. (Reaney s.n. Moor, MED s.v. mōr (n. (1)))
    John de Mora 1274 V1 p83
    John de la More 1275 V1 p126
    Matthew del, de More, Mora 1275 V1 p118, 120
    Philip de Mora 1275 V1 p138
    Robert de la More 1275 V1 p130

Morehous
There are many places in the West Riding modernly called Moorhouse or Moor House. The name means "house on the moor or marsh," and is from OE *mōr* + *hūs*. (Reaney s.n. Moorhouse, Smith viii.126)
    William del Morehous junior 1350 V6 p3
    Richard del Morehous 1351 V6 p46
    William del Morehous 1351 V6 p36, 60

Moreman
"One who lives by the marsh," from OE **mōrmann* "marsh-dweller." (Reaney s.n. Moorman)
    William Moreman 1350 V6 p4

Morthyng
Modern Morthen. "Moor assembly place," from OE *mōr* or ON *mór* + OE, ON *þing* "assembly, council." (Smith vii.65, 225, 259)
    William de Morthyng 1274 V1 p92

Mortimer
From Mortemer, in Normandy. (Reaney s.n. Mortimer)
    Robert Mortimer 1351 V6 p23

Moscroft
Modern Molescroft, in the East Riding. "Mul's enclosure," or "mule's field," from either the OE personal name *Mūl* + *croft*, or OE *mūl*, ON *múll* "mule" + *croft*. (Smith ERY 200; Watts s.n. Molescroft)
    Ralph de Moscroft 1275 V1 p150

Neubiggen
Modern New Biggin Hill or one of the other places that bore this name. "The new building," from OE *nīwe* + ME *bigging*. Smith says this is "a common type of (place name) in the north," and indeed, there are several small places named New Biggin or similar. (Smith iii.108)
    Adam del Neubiggen, Neubigging, Neubiggeng 1274
        V1 p99, 137

Neuriding
I am not sure what this place name is, but the name probably means "new clearing," from OE *nīwe* + **rydding* "clearing." (Smith vii.228, 238)
    John de Neuriding 1275 V1 p152

Neusom
Modern Newsome. "(At) the new houses," from OE *nīwe* + *hūs* + *-um*. (Smith ii.258)
    Robert de Neusom 1275 V1 p119

Neuton
Modern Newton, "new farmstead," from OE *nīwe* + *tūn*. (Smith ii.156)
    Gemme de Neuton 1275 V1 p133

Neville
From a French place name, either Néville or Neuville. (Reaney s.n. Nevill)
    Geoffrey de Neville 1274 V1 p84

Northcliff
Modern North Cliffe. "North bank," from OE *norð* + *clif*. (Smith iii.92)
    John de Northcliff, Northclif 1350 V6 p5, 8

Northend
"From the north end (of the village, hill, etc.)." From OE *norð* + *ende*. (Reaney s.n. Northend)
    John del Northend 1351 V6 p22

Northland
Modern Norland, "north stretch of land," from OE *norð* + *land*.
    Alan de Northland 1274 V1 p80
    John de Northland, Norlaund 1274 V1 p94, 146
    William de Northlaund, Norlaund, Norland 1274 V1 p101, 126, 136
    William de Northlaund 1274 V1 p101 Listed as "Another William de Northlaund," immediately after the other one.
    Adam de Norland 1275 V1 p142
    Hugh de Norlaund 1275 V1 p117
    Richard de Northland 1351 V6 p55

Northmanton

Modern Normanton. "Farmstead of the Norwegians," from OE *Norðmann* + *tūn*. (Smith ii.121)

    Henry de Normanton, Northmanton 1275 V1 p143, 154

    Geoffrey de Northmanton 1275 V1 p132

Northuuerum

Modern Northowram, meaning "on the north slope" (Northowram and Southowram are two ridges in the area, between which runs Shibden Brook.) From OE *æt uferum*, *ufer* being a variant of *ofer*, "a slope, hill, ridge." (Smith iii.89, 96)

    Adam de Northouerum, Northuuerum 1274 V1 p81

    Jordan de Northuuerum 1274 V1 p81 (Probably same as Jordan son of Thomas de Northuuerum mentioned in following paragraph.)

    Richard de Northouerum 1274 V1 p80

    Roger de Northuuerum 1274 V1 p81

    Thomas de Northuuerum 1274 V1 p81

    Henry de Northouerum 1275 V1 p113

Northwode

"One who lives north of the woods" or in one of the places modernly called Northwood or Norwood. From OE *norð* + *wudu*. (Reaney s.n. Northwood)

    Ivo de Northwode 1274 V1 p96

    John del Northwod 1352 V6 p92

Northwyche

Possibly Northwich in Cheshire, or a "dweller at the north saltworks" from OE *north* + *wīc* "a collection of buildings for a particular purpose." (Watts s.n. Northwich)

    Philip de Northwyche, Northwych 1352 V6 p75, 77

Nuteschawe

Nutshaw is a place in Lancashire, near Burnley. The name means "copse where nuts are grown," from OE *hnutu* + *sceaga*. (Ekwall *Lancashire* 136, Smith vii.205, 240)

    John de Nuteschawe, Noteschawe 1275 V1 p109

    William de Nuteschawe, Noteschawe, Notesahe 1350 V6 p5

Okes

There are several places in the West Riding called Oaks or The Oaks; the meaning is, of course, "oak trees," from OE *āc*. (Smith iii.72, Reaney s.n. Oak)

    Henry de Okes 1350 V6 p7

    Thomas del Okes 1351 V6 p60

Oldfeld

"One who lives by the old field," from OE *eald* + *feld*. (Reaney s.n. Oldfield)

    William del Oldfeld 1350 V6 p5

    Roger del Oldfeld 1351 V6 p40

Ossett

Modern Ossett. Probably "fold frequented by thrushes," from OE *ōsle* "thrush" + *(ge)set* "dwelling, camp, fold," but the first element is possibly an OE personal name, *Ōsla*, so this could also be "Ōsla's fold." (Smith ii.188)

    Henry de Osset, Ossett 1275 V1 p109, 129

    Serlo de Ossett 1275 V1 p120

    Richard de Ossett 1350 V6 p16, 88

    John de Ossett 1351 V6 p22

    Richard de Ossett of Walton, Osset of Walton 1352 V6 p83, 87

(Walton is another local place name, meaning "farmstead of the Welshmen or serfs," from OE *Walh* [genitive plural of Wala] + *tūn*.)

Otlay
Modern Otley. (Reaney s.n. Otley)
    John de Otlay 1352 V6 p91 servant

Ouerum
Modern Northowram, Southowram, or just a name meaning "on the slopes" (Northowram and Southowram are two ridges in the area, between which runs Shibden Brook.) From OE *æt uferum*, *ufer* being a variant of *ofer*, "a slope, hill, ridge." (Smith iii.96, 89)
    Adam de Ouerum 1274 V1 p81
    (Possibly the same as Adam de Northouerum on the same page)

Ovenden
Modern Ovenden. Smith suggests two origins: one from OE *ofen* "furnace" + *denu* "valley," and the other more probable origin from OE *ofan*, *ufan* "over, above" + *denu*. (Smith iii.113)
    Hugh de Ovenden 1275 v1 p104
    John de Ovenden 1275 V1 p125
    Ralph de Ovenden 1275 v1 p104
    William de Ovenden 1275 V1 p125
    Adam de Ovynden, Ovenden 1350 V6 p12, 86
    Alexander de Ovynden 1351 V6 p23
    John de Ovynden 1351 V6 p48

Overhalle
"One who lives by or at the upper hall." (Reaney s.n. Overal)
>John del Overhalle, Overhall 1350 V6 p1, 37

Pendaunt
"One who lives on a slope," from Anglo-French *pendaunt*. (MED s.v. pendaunt (n.), Reaney s.n. Pendant)
>Richard del Pendant, Pondant, Pendaunt 1274 V1 p85, 89, 152
>Margery del Pendaunt (f) 1275 V1 p118

Plegwyk
Modern Pledwick. Probably "a place where games or sports were played," from OE *plega* "play, sports, game" + *wīc*, "hamlet, farmstead, building." (Smith ii.108)
>John de Plegwyk 1350 V6 p2

Presteley
Modern Priestley Green. "Priests' clearing," from OE *prēost* + *lēah*. (Smith iii.80)
>Richard de Presteley, Prestlay 1275 V1 p112, 123

Querneby
Modern Quarmby. "Farmstead with a mill," from ON *kvern* + *bȳ*.
>John de Querneby 1274 V1 p83, 85 87
>Adam de Querneby 1275 V1 p142

Quickeleden
Modern Wickleden, cited in the Wakefield Rolls in 1699 as Whickleden. "Quick-set hedge hill valley," from OE *cwic* + *hyll* + *denu*. (Smith ii.248)

Henry de Quickeleden 1275 V1 p118
Cecilia de Qwycleden (f) 1352 V6 p106

Quallay
Modern Whalley in Lancashire. "Clearing on or near a round hill," from OE *hwæl* + *lēah*. (Mills s.n. Whalley; Ekwall *Lancashire* 76)
William de Qwallay, Quallay 1350 V6 p7, 68, 75

Rachedale
Modern Rochdale, in Lancashire (now in Greater Manchester). From the name of the river Roch + OScand *dalr*, however, the river's name itself is a back-formation from the town's earlier name, *Recedham*, from OE *reced* "hall" + *ham* "homestead." (Mills, s.n. Rochdale; Ekwall *Lancashire* 54)
Henry de Rachedale 1275 V1 p139
Marjory de Rachedale (f) 1275 V1 p129
Amora de Rachedale (f) 1351 V6 p17
Henry de Rachedale 1351 V6 p40

Rastrik
Modern Rastrick. Smith suggests it is a compound of ON *rǫst* "resting-place" and OE *ric* "a narrow strip or track," meaning "a road with a resting place." The location is appropriate to this interpretation, being on the main road from Brighouse to Rochdale in Lancashire, which followed the old Roman road. (Smith iii.38)
Hugh de Rastrik 1274 V1 p95
Reymund de Rastrik 1274 V1 p81
Roger de Rastrik 1274 V1 p85
John de Rastrik, Rastrick 1274 V1 p86, 87, 145
Ellen de Rastrik (f) 1350 V6 p7

John de Rastrik 1350 V6 p7
Matilda de Rastrik (f) 1350 V6 p7

Ravenesfeud
Modern Ravenfield, "Raven's open land." The first element may be OE *hræfn* or ON *hrafn* (both "raven"), or a personal name derived from either of those words. The second element is OE *feld*, "open land." (Smith i.172)
    John de Ravenesfeud 1274 V1 p83, 84. 85, 86, 150
        "Bailiff of the Earl (of Warren)"

Rediker
Modern Redacre Wood, or another "reedy marsh," from OE *hrēodig* + ON *kjarr*. (Smith iii.161)
    Richard del Rediker 1275 V1 p152
    Alice del Redykar, Redykerre, Rodyker (f) 1352 V6
        p71, 91, 43

Richemond
Modern Richmond, of which there is one in the North Riding and one in the West Riding. "Strong hill" from OFr *riche* + *mont*. (Smith i.165)
    Thomas de Richemond 1351 V6 p61

Ridyng
"One who lives in a cleared area," from OE **rydding*. (Reaney s.n. Reading, MED s.v. ridding(e (ger.))
    Henry atte, del Ridyng 1274 V1 p80, 93
    William del Ryding 1350 V6 p4

Roaldesete
I am not sure what this name is. I note that Roaldset is a modern Norwegian surname. Perhaps this is Norse, maybe "Roald's Seat," from the name *Roald* + ON *sǽti* "seat,

outcrop of rock resembling a seat" or also "a residence." Alternatively, the second element may be from ON *sǽtr*, "mountain pasture, shieling." (Smith vii.239, MED s.v. recoilen (v.) where the name Roald is cited, Smith *English Place Name Elements* ii.95)

    John de Roaldesete 1274 V1 p93
    Thomas de Roaldesete 1274 V1 p93

Rode, Rodes

"One who lives by the clearing." This is the element that, in the Yorkshire dialect, later became typically "Royd." From OE *rod(u)*. (Reaney s.n. Rhodes)

    Alan del Rodes 1274 V1 p89
    Richard del, de Rode, Rodes 1274 V1 p82, 98, 103, 120
    Henry del Rode 1275 V1 p112
    Thomas del Rode 1275 V1 p114, 126
    William del Rode 1350 V6 p8
    John del Rod, Rode 1351 V6 p1, 22, 76
    Richard del Rode 1351 V6 p23, 60
    Alice del Rodes (f) 1351 V6 p59
    Adam del Rode 1352 V6 p68
    Henry del Rodes 1352 V6 p89

Rokes

"Of the oaks." The "r" was sometimes used, sometimes not; e.g. ME *atter oke*, *atte roke*, both meaning "at the oak." (Reaney s.n. Roke)

    Jordan del Rokis, Rokes 1275 V1 p112, 123

Rollesby

Modern Rollesby, in Norfolk. "Hrólfr's farmstead," from the ON personal name *Hrólfr* + ON *bȳ*. (Mills s.n. Rollesby)

> William de Rollesby 1274 y Sir V1 p91

Romesden

Modern Ramsden. Probably "valley of the ram," from OE *ramm* + *denu*, but the first element may possibly be OE *hramsa* "wild garlic" or an OE personal name, *Ramm*. (Smith ii.237)

> Matthew de Romesden, de Romesdene, Romesden (without the "de"), Romesdon 1350 V6 p1, 12, 13, 50, 97

Routh

Modern Routh, in the East Riding. Possibly from ON *hrúðr*, "rough, shaly ground." (Mills s.n. Routh, Smith ERY 71)

> Peter de Routh, Routhe 1351 V6 p36, 100

Routonstal

Modern Rawtonstall. "Rough farmstead," from OE *rūh* + *tūn-stall*. (Smith iii.197)

> William de Routonstall 1274 V1 p93
> Michael de Routonstal 1275 V1 p116

Rylay

Modern Riley. "Clearing used for growing rye," from OE *rȳge* + *lēah*. (Smith ii.246)

> Robert de Rylay 1351 V6 p47

Rysshewrth
Modern Rishworth. "Enclosure among or growing with rushes," from OE *risc* + *worð*. (Smith iii.71)
    Elias de Richewrt 1275 V1 p124
    Henry de Rissewrth, 1275 V1 p108, 116
    Henry de Rysshewrth 1351 V6 p55
    Nicholas de Rysshewrth 1352 V6 p89

Saltonstall
Modern Saltonstall. "Farmstead near the willow," from OE *salh* "willow" + *tūn-stall*. (Smith iii.125)
    William de Saltonestall, Saltonstal 1274 V1 p80, 147
    Robert de Saltunstal, Saltonstal, Saltonstall 1275 V1 p116, 117, 147
    William de Saltonstall 1350 V6 p4, 43, 93
    Thomas de Saltonstall, of Saltonstall, Saltenstall 1351 V6 p44, 48, 76
    John de Saltonstall 1352 V6 p93

Saltthwayth
This appears at first glance to be "salt clearing," from OE *salt* + ON *þveit*. This may be the origin, but I have not found a modern Salthwaite or anything similar. There is, however, a Slaithwaite. The historical spellings cited for that place are similar, and the village is in the right area, but none of the spellings begin with Sal- so there's no direct indication that it is related. (Smith ii.307)
    Robert de Saltthwayth, Salttheweyt 1275 V1 p116 "living at Querneby"

Sandale
Modern Sandal Magna. "Sandy nook of land," from OE *sand* + *halh*. Another similar name in the area is Kirk

Sandall, also sometimes known as simply Sandale. The etymology is the same. (Smith ii.107)
    Philipot de Sandale 1350 V6 p15
    James de Sandale 1351 V6 p40
    Robert de Sandale 1352 V6 p77

Santinglay
Modern Santingley, possibly "a place cleared by burning," from OE *senget* "a place cleared by burning" + *lēah* "forest-glade or clearing." (Smith i.262)
    Robert de Santinglay, Santynglay 1352 V6 p87, 95

Santon
Modern Sancton (which was in the East Riding). "Farm or village on sand," from OE *sand* + *tūn*. (Watts s.n. Sancton, Smith ERY 227)
    Peter de Santon 1275 v1 p104

Sayton
There are several modern Seatons; this may be the one in the East Riding, meaning "farm, village, or estate near the sea" (in this case, a lake), from OE *sǣ* + *tūn*. (Watts s.n. Seaton, Smith ERY 67)
    William de Sayton, Seyton, also without the *de*. 1351
        V6 p43, 48, 75

Sayvill
Reaney suggests this is a locative from Sauville (Ardennes, Vosges) or Sainville (Eure-et-Loir). (Reaney s.n. Savil; see also W. Paley Baildon, "Notes on the early Saville pedigree and the Butlers of Skelbrook and Kirk Sandal," Sections I and II, *Yorkshire Archaeological Journal*, vol. 28, pp. 380-419, 1926, viewable online at

http://www.medievalgenealogy.org.uk/sources/saville/baild on1.shtml.)
 Baldwin de Seyville, Sayville, Seyvile, Ceyville 1274
  V1 p83, 85, 92, 127, 140: on p. 140, "le Sceyville"
 Henry Sayvill 1352 V6 p87

Schakeltonstal
Modern Shackleton in the parish of Halifax. Either "farmstead where animals could be tied up," from OE *sceacol*, or "stubble farmstead," from OE *sceacel + *tūn-stall*. (Smith iii.201, Redmonds *English Surnames* 76)
 Elkoc, Alkoc de Schakeltonstal, Chakeltonstell 1274
  V1 p81, 143
 Jordan de Schakeltonstal, Schakeltonstall, Saltonstall
  (possibly in error) 1274 V1 p81, 86, 89, 107
 William de Schakeltonstall 1274 V1 p100

Shagh
"One who lives in a wood or forest." From OE *sceaga*, *scaga*. (MED s.v. shau(e (n.), Reaney s.n. Shaw)
 Henry del Sagh, Shaghe, Shagh 1351, 1352 V6 p43,
  79, 82
 Roger del Schaw 1351 V6 p23

Schefeld
Modern Sheffield. "Open countryside by the river Sheaf," from OE *scēath* + fe*l*d. (Watts s.n. Sheffield, Smith i.204)
 Ralph de Schefeld, Schefeud, Chefeud, Sefeud 1274
  V1 p83, 86, 87, 137, 141

Schelf
Modern Shelf. "The shelf or ledge," from OE *scelf*. (Watts s.n. Shelf)
    Elias de Schelf 1275 V1 p112
    Thomas de Schelf 1275 V1 p113

Schelfley
Modern Shelley. "Glade or clearing on a shelving terrain," from OE *scelf* + *lēah*. (Smith ii.249)
    Robert de Schelfley 1274 V1 p89
    Elias de Schelfley 1275 V1 p143

Schelton
Modern Shelton (of which there are several, including one in Nottingham). "Settlement on or by a shelf of land." from OE *scelf* + *tūn*. (Reaney s.n. Shelton, Watts s.n. Shelton)
    Roger de Schelton 1275 V1 p156

Schepeley
Modern Shepley, "sheep clearing." From OE *scēap* + *lēah*. (Smith ii.250, Watts s.n. Shepley)
    Walter de Schepeley 1274 V1 p80
    Agnes de Schepele (f) 1275 V1 p109
    John de Schepley 1275 V1 p120

Schipeden
Modern Shibden, "sheep valley," from OE *scēap* + *denu*. (Smith iii.92)
    William de Schipeden, Schypeden 1274 V1 p90 96
    Hugh de Schipeden 1275 V1 p145

Sckyrecote
Modern Skircoat. "Bright cottage," from OE *scīr*

(influenced by ON *skírr*) + *cot*. (Smith iii.110)
    Elias de Sckyrecote, Schyrecote 1274 V1 p86 89

Scoles
Modern Scholes. "The sheds or shielings," from ON *skáli*. (Smith ii.247)
    John del Scoles 1275 V1 p119
    Matthew del Scolis, Scoles 1275 V1 p106, 148
    Peter del Scoles 1275 V1 p112
    Richard del Scoles 1275 V1 p148
    Simon de Scolis 1275 V1 p106
    Hugh del Scoles 1350 V6 p3
    John del, de Skoles 1350 V6 p8, 15

Shaghlay
Modern Shaley. "Clearing by the copse," from OE *sceaga* + *lēah*. (Smith ii.254)
    Robert de Shaghlay 1350 V6 p16

Shee
I am not sure if this is "One who lives by the wood," from OE *sceaga*, *scaga*; the spelling "shee" seems untypical. (MED s.v. shau(e (n.), Reaney s.n. Shaw)
    William del Shee 1352 V6 p71

Shellay
Modern Shelley. "Glade or clearing on a shelving terrain," from OE *scelf* + *lēah*. (Smith ii.249)
    Christiana de Shellay (f)1351 V6 p59
    Thomas de Shellay 1351 V6 p29

Shirclif
Modern Shirecliffe Hall, in Sheffield. "The bright steep hillside," from OE *scīr* + *clif*. (Reaney s.n. Shercliff, Smith i.212)
    Margery de Shirclif (f) 1350 V6 p1

Shore
"One who lives by the shore." (Reaney s.n. Shore)
    John del Shore 1352 V6 p75
    Margery del Shore (f)1352 V6 p91
    Matilda del Shore (f) 1352 V6 p71

Skulcote
From Sculcoates in the East Riding. "Skúli's cottage," from the ON personal name *Skúli* + OE *cote*. (Watts s.n. Sculthorpe, Reaney s.n. School, MED s.v. cōt(e (n. (1)), Dixon, Smith ERY 214)
    William de Sculecote, Sculecotes 1275 v1 p105, 147
    Richard de Skulcote 1350 V6 p2
    John de Skulcote 1352 V6 p90

Slac
"One who lives in the shallow valley," from ON *slakki*. (Reaney s.n. Slack, MED s.v. slak (n.(2)))
    Thomas del Slac 1275 V1 p105, 150 of Querneby
    William del Slak 1350 V6 p4

Slaneden
I am not sure what place name this is, but the second element is most likely OE *denu*, "valley."
    John de Slaneden 1351 V6 p40, 44

Smallegh
Modern Small Lees. "Narrow clearings," from OE *smæl* + *lēah*. (Smith iii.65)
    Agnes Smallegh (f) 1352 V6 p92

Snape
Several places in the West Riding carry the name Snape. This may be from one of them, or just a general snape, "a boggy piece of land" from OE *snæp*, or "poor pasture-land" from ON *snap*. (Reaney s.n. Snape, Smith iii.149, MED s.v. snape (n.))
    Hugh del Snape 1352 V6 p92

Snayppethorp
Modern Snapethorp. "Sneypi's outlying farmstead," from the ON name *Sneypir* "one who pinches" + *þorp*. (Smith ii.155)
    Torald de Snayppethorp 1275 V1 p132
    Henry de Snaypthorp 1275 V1 p140

Soland
Modern Soyland, possibly "slough land" from OE *sol* "mud, slough" + *land* "district, stretch of land." (Smith iii.62)
    Alice de Soland (f) 1274 V1 p136
    Henry de Soland 1274 V1 p80
    Ivo de Soland, Solaund 1274 V1 p80, 116
    Philip de Soland 1275 V1 p152

Sothill
Modern Lower Soothill, "soot hill." from OE *sōt* + *hyll*. (Smith ii.193, 197)
    Matthew de Sothil 1275 V1 p146
    Michael de Sothill 1275 V1 p152

John de Sothill 1350 V6 p2
Johanna de Sothill (f) 1351 V6 p42

Sourby
Modern Sowerby Bridge. "Farmstead on sour ground," from ON *saurr* "mud, dirt, sour land" + *by* "farmstead." (Smith iii.144)
Hayne de Soureby 1274 V1 p91
Malyna de Soureby (f) 1274 V1 p97
Nelle de Soureby 1274 V1 p90
Robert de Soureby, Sourby 1274 V1 p80, 147
Soyer, Seyer de Soureby 1274 V1 p80, 109
Alan de Sourby 1275 V1 p114
Alkoc de Sourby 1275 V1 p117
John de Sourby 1350 V6 p6
Robert de Sourby 1351 V6 p28, 44
William de Sourby 1351 V6 p56

Southourom
Modern Southowram. "On the (south) slopes," from OE *æt uferum*. (Smith iii.89)
Beatrice de Southourom (f) 1350 V6 p8

Southwod
Possibly modern Southwood field, or another "south wood." OE *suð* + *wudu*. (Smith iii.39, Reaney s.n. Southwood)
Adam de Southwod 1351 V6 p29

St. Oswald[+]
The medieval church of St. Oswald's is in Sowerby, near Thirsk, in North Yorkshire. This is not the same place as Sowerby Bridge, near Halifax. I cannot find any village of

this name, however. ("History of St Oswald")

    Isolda de Sancto Osewaldo (f) 1275 v1 p103

Stable+

"Of the Stable." Probably an occupational name, though it is also locative.

    Johannes de Stabulo 1275 V1 p144 The translator gives this as "del Stabulo" which is possibly a mistranscription of the Latin version, or perhaps the Latin version has a typo; later Rolls seem to have the name del Stable, so I am listing this under that vernacular name.

Stakwod

Smith discusses modern Stagwood Hill, which is cited in the Wakefield Rolls in 1307 as *Stackwodeker* and in 1454 as *Stackwodd bancke*. This does seem to refer to the ME compound of *stak* and *wode*; as it seems to be a place name, it is a likely candidate for the location of *Stakwod*. (Smith ii.241, MED s.vv. stak (n.), wōde (n.(2)))

    Robert de Stakwod 1352 V6 p97

Stanclif

Modern Stonecliff Lodge, Staincliffe, or Stancliffe. ON *steinn* "stone" + OE *clif* or ON *klif* "cliff." (Smith ii.181, 207, 227)

    Henry de Stanclif 1274 V1 p87
    Hugh de Stanclif, Staneclyf, Stanclyf 1274 V1 p96, 147, 150, 151
    John de Stanclif 1274 V1 p80 96

Stanley

Modern Stanley. "Stony clearing," from OE *stān* + *lēah*. (Smith ii.159)

Thomas de Stanley 1274 V1 p90
Walter de Stanley 1274 V1 p87
William de Stanley, Staneley 1274 V1 p92, 147
Anot de Stanley (f)1275 V1 p117
Ralph de Stanley 1275 V1 p131

Stansfeld
Modern Stansfield. Smith suggests that there are some questions about the origin of this name, and that the commonly cited meaning "Stān's open field" may not apply to this West Riding place name. He suggests that ON *stanes* + *feld*, meaning either "open land marked by a stone" or "open land belonging to a place called *Stān*," is a more plausible origin, and notes that the site is in fact marked by a large stone or stones. (Smith iii.178, Watts s.n. Stansfield.)
William de Stansfeld 1350 V6 p4, 42

Staynclif
Modern Stonecliff Lodge, Staincliffe, or Stancliffe. ON *steinn* "stone" + OE *clif* or ON *klif* "cliff." (Smith ii.181, 207, 227)
John de Staynclif, Staynclyff 1351 V6 p8, 22
Adam de Stayncliff, Steynclif 1352 V6 p69, 100

Staynland
Modern Stainland. "Stony stretch of land," OE *stān* (later ON steinn) + OE *land*. (Smith vii.49)
Thomas de Stanland, Staynland 1275 V1 p140, 146

Stelyng
Reaney suggests this name is from one of two place names (the Northumberland one being the more likely here). Watts mentions a possible OE **stelling* meaning "stall

place, cattle fold" which could possibly relate to this name. (Reaney s.n. Stelling, Watts s.n. Stelling Minnis)
> William Stelyng 1274 V1 p100

Stert
See *Stert* in the nicknames section of this appendix.
> Henry Stert 1275 V1 p131

Stevenrod
Modern Stephen Royd. "Stephen's clearing," from the ME personal name *Stephen* + OE *rod*. (Smith 4 153)
> Richard del Stevenrod 1352 V6 p80

Stockes
Reaney suggests this is "one who lives by the tree stumps" (or, in some cases, by a foot bridge). This is quite probably an actual West Riding place, modernly Stocks, the name of which does refer to a place with tree stumps. OE *stocc*. (MED s.vv. stok (n. (1)), Reaney s.n. Stock, Smith ii.252)
> Richard del Stockes 1275 V1 p105
> Robert del Stokkis, Stokis 1275 V1 p112, 116
> John del Stockes 1351 V6 p58
> Nicholas del Stockes, Stookes 1352 V6 p84, 102

Stodley
Modern Stoodley. "Clearing used as a stud." OE *stōd* + *lēah*. (Smith iii.178)
> Henry de Stodley 1274 V1 p93
> William de Stodley 1274 V1 p93
> William de Stodelay 1350 V6 p15

Storthes
Modern Storthes Hall. "The plantations," from ON *storð*. (Smith ii.252)

Matthew de Stordes 1275 V1 p120
William del, de Storthes 1350 V6 p2, 58

Sugden
Modern Sugden End or another of the Sugden place names in the area. "Boggy valley," from OE *sugga* "swamp, bog" + *denu*. (Smith iii.262).
Hugh de Sugden 1351 V6 p44

Sundreland
Modern High Sunderland in Northowram, "private land," from OE *sundor* + *land*. (Reaney s.n. Sunderland)
Alcok, Alkoc de Sundreland, Sondreland, Sunderland 1274 V1 p85, 89, 147
Mathew de Sundreland 1274 V1 p80
Henry de Sonderland 1352 V6 p69

Suthclif
Modern Sutcliff Wood. "South cliff or bank," from OE *sūð* + *clif*. (Smith iii.77)
Hugh de Suthclif 1274 V1 p82, 85

Suthorp
Southorpe in the East Riding. From OE *sūð* + ON *þorp*. (Smith, *Place Names of the East Riding*, 65)
Robert de Suthorp 1274 V1 p91

Swylington
Modern Swillington. Possibly "the settlement at Swinling," meaning "swine hill" (from OE *swīn* + *hyll* + *tūn)* or "swine pasture place" (from OE *swīn* + *lēah* + *tūn*). (Watts s.n. Swillington)
Henry de Swylington 1275 V1 p106

Swynesheved
Modern Swineshead, "swine head," from OE *swīn* + *hēafod*. (Smith iii.179)
William de Swynesheved 1274 V1 p82

Syk'
One who lives near a small stream. The apostrophe here denotes a scribal abbreviation for a name that was probably a form of *Sykes*. (Reaney s.n. Sykes)
Richard del Syk' 1275 V1 p105

Tetlawe
Modern Tetlow, in Lancashire. "Tetta's hill," from OE *Tetta* + *hlāw*. (Ekwall *Lancashire* 33)
Hugh de Tetlawe 1352 V6 p73

Thirsk
Modern Thirsk. Located in the North Riding. "Lake or fen," from ON **thresk*. (Watts s.n. Thirsk.)
John de Thirsk 1352 V6 p68 John de Thirsk chaplain

Thomil
This is possibly a misreading of Thornil or Thornhil, though there are a couple of Tom Hills in the West Riding (cited by Smith at later dates). The place, modern Thornhill, means "thorn-tree hill," from OE *þorn* + *hyll*. See Thornhill, below. (Smith ii.210)
Thomas de Thomil V1 p129

Thorn'
Probably Thornes (typically referred to in this record as *Spinetum*, but that is a Latin translation of the vernacular). "The thorn-trees," from OE *þorn*. (Smith ii.168)
John de Thorn' 1274 V1 p89

Thorneleye, Thornyley
Modern Thornleigh. "Thorny clearing,," from OE *þornig* + *lēah*. (Smith ii.299)
    Nelle del Thorneleye, Thornyley 1274 V1 p100, 102

Thornes
Modern Thornes (typically referred to in this record as Spinetum, but that is a Latin translation of the vernacular). "The thorn-trees," from OE *þorn*. (Smith ii.168)
    Magge de Thornes (f) 1274 V1 p96

Thornetlay
I am not sure which modern place this may be, but it is probably "thorn copse clearing," from OE *þornett* + *lēah* or "thorny clearing" from *þorniht* + *lēah*; Smith mentions a field name, *Thornetelay*. (Smith vii.260).
    Cecilia de Thornetlay (f) 1351 V6 p61
    John de Thornetlay 1351 V6 p18

Thorneton
Modern Thornton. "Farmstead or enclosure among the thorn-trees," from OE þorn + tūn. (Smith iii.271)
    Thomas de Thorneton 1274 V1 p85

Thornhill
Modern Thornhill, "thorn-tree hill," from OE *þorn* + *hyll*. See Thomil above. (Smith ii.210)
    Richard de Thornhyll, Thornhill, Thornil, Thornhil
        1274 V1 p81, 86, 87, 89, 107, 141
    Thomas de Thornhill 1275 V1 p146

Thorniceley
I am not sure what this is, unless it is a mistake for

Thornetelay.
    William de Thorniceley 1275 V1 p120

Thornyales
According to Smith, this is modern Thornhills, "Thorny nooks of land," from OE *þornig* + *halh*, but Faull and Moorhouse suggest it may also be from a lost field-name in Rastrick. (Smith iii.4; Faull and Moorhouse, *West Yorkshire, an Archaeological Survey to 1500*, 1981, West Yorkshire Metropolitan County Council, p. 348)
    Roger de Thornyales 1350 V6 p8

Thorp
There are multiple Thorpes, including modern Thorpe on the Hill. "Outlying farmstead," from ON *þorp*. (Smith ii.149)
    Peter de Thorp 1275 V1 p105
    Richard del Thorp, Thorpe 1350 V6 p8, 83

Thothyll
Modern Toothill. "Look-out hill," from OE *tōt-hyll*. (Smith iii.40)
    Richard de Thothyll 1274 V1 p80
    Henry de Totil 1275 V1 p113

Thurstanland
Modern Thurstonland. "Thurstan's expanse of land," from the ON personal name *Þorsteinn* or ODan *Thorsten, Þursten* + OE *land*. (Smith ii.251)
    Margery de Thurstanland (f) 1275 V1 p139

Thwong

Modern Upperthong, or nearby Netherthong (both were cited with the "Thoung" spelling in this period). "A narrow strip of land," from OE *þwang* "thong." (Smith ii.286, 288)

>John de Thwong 1274 V1 p97
>Robert de Thwong 1274 V1 p99
>William de Thweng, Thwong 1274 V1 p82, 97
>Nicholas de Thoung 1275 V1 p118
>Thomas de Thoung 1275 V1 p113
>Geoffrey de Thwong 1350 V6 p2
>Simon de Thwong 1350 V6 p2

Toun

"Of the village, the town." (Reaney s.n. Town)

>Thomas del Toun 1352 V6 p104

Trimingham

Modern Trimmingham. Smith suggests that the name originated from Trimingham, Norfolk, and was then a manorial name derived from a particular family, which then became the place name in the West Riding. "Home of Trymma's folk." (Smith iii.111)

>William de Trimigham, Trimingham 1274 V1 p83, 114

Turnay

From Tournai, Tournay, or Tourny, in Normandy. (Reaney s.n. Turney)

>Thomas Turnay, de Turnay, de Tournay 1351 V6 p59, 17

Uchethorp

Modern Ouchthorpe. Probably "garden farmstead," from OFr *(h)ouche* "garden" + ON *þorp*. (Smith ii.157)

Philip de Uchethorp 1274 V1 p92
Ralph de Uchethorp 1274 V1 p90
William de Uchethorp 1275 V1 p124

Undrewode
One who lives "under the wood" (that is, below a wood on a hillside, or perhaps below the trees in a wood). (Reaney s.n. Underwood)
John Undrewode, Underwode 1275 V1 p56, 60

Undreclif
One who lives below a cliff or slope. (Reaney s.n. Undercliff)
Thomas Undreclif 1274 V1 p80

Waddeswrth
Modern Wadsworth Moor. "Wæddi's enclosure," from an OE personal name in the genitive + *worð*. (Watts s.n. Wadsworth Moor, Smith iii.199)
Adam de Waddiswrth, Waddeswrth 1274 V1 p85 90
John de Waddiswrth 1275 V1 p153
Adam de Waddeswrth 1351 V6 p43
John de Waddeswrth 1351 V6 p24
Richard of Waddeswrth 1351 V6 p25

Wakefeud
Wakefield. The *-feud* spelling is very common in the Rolls during this period. (Smith ii.163)
Nigel de Wakefeud 1274 V1 p85
William de Wakefeud 1274 V1 p92

Wales
Wales, in this case, is unlikely to be the country, but instead

the West Riding location called Wales. (Smith ii.155)
    John de Wales 1351 V6 p56

Wallay
Probably a locative, from Whalley in nearby Lancashire. "Clearing by the hill." From OE *hwæl* + *lēah*. But see also Wollay, below. (Reaney s.n. Whalley; Ekwall *Lancashire* 76; Watts s.n. Whalley.)
    Thomas de Wallay 1350 V6 p2
    Hugh Wallay 1352 V6 p87

Walton
Modern Walton. "Farmstead of the Welshmen or serfs," from OE *Walh* + *tūn*. (Smith ii.112.)
    Peter de Waleton, Walton 1274 V1 p83, 102
    Hugh de Walton 1275 V1 p102
    Peter de Walton 1275 V1 p102
    Serlo de Walton 1275 V1 p129
    William de Walton 1352 V6 p77

Wambewell
Modern Wombwell. Possibly "Wamba's spring," from OE personal name **Wamba* + *wella*. **Wamba*, if it existed (there are parallel names in OHG and possibly in ON) may be from OE *wamb*, "womb or belly," and it is also possible that this is the direct origin of Wombwell, with "womb" used in a figurative topographical sense such as a hollow or a lake. (Smith i.102, Watts s.n. Wombwell)
    Robert de Wambewell, Wambewelle 1275 V1 p102, 107

Welle
"One who lives by a spring." (Reaney s.n. Atwell)
    Roger atte Welle 1350 V6 p7

Welles

Probably "one who lived near a group of springs." (Reaney s.n. Wells)

    John de Welles 1351 V6 p20

Werloweley

Modern Warley. "Werlaf's glade or clearing," from an OE personal name *Wērlāf* + *lēah*. (Smith iii.122.)

    Adam de Warloweley, Werloweley 1274 V1 p80, 94
    William de Werloley 1275 V1 p152
    Jordan de Werloweley V1 p108 "fined 6d for chattering in Court" — "*pro multiloquio in Curia, finivit vjd.*"
    Ivo de Werloweley, Werloley 1274 V1 p80

West

"One from the west." (Reaney s.n. West)

    William del West 1352 V6 p100

Western

Despite the question mark in the transliteration, this probably is indeed "Western," meaning one from the west. There are others of this name mentioned in slightly later editions of the Rolls. (Reaney s.n. Western.)

    Alice le Western (?) (f) 1275 V1 p127

Westwod

"One who lives by the west wood." See also *Estwode*, above. (Reaney s.n. Westwood)

    Thomas de Westwod 1274 V1 p93

Whetlay

Modern Wheatley. "Clearing used for growing wheat,"

from OE *hwǣte* + *lēah*. (Smith i.36)
    Edmund de Whetlay 1352 V6 p85

Whitacre
"White field," from OE *hwīt* + *æcer* or possibly a similar ON form. Probably modern High Whitaker, in Padiham, Lancashire, not terribly far away from the Wakefield area. (Ekwall *Lancashire* 80; Reaney s.n. Whitaker.)
    Thomas de Whitacre 1350 V6 p7

Whithill
"White, bright hill," from OE *hwīt* + *hyll*. There are several places of this name both here and in Lancashire. (Smith iii.116, i.42; Reaney s.n. Whittle; Ekwall ODEPN s.n. Whittle)
    John de Whitill, Whithill 1350 V6 p12, 69

Whitlygh
"White, bright clearing, " from OE *hwīt* + *lēah*. This is a very common place name in the West Riding, and modern spellings of these place names include Whitley, White Lee, and Whiteley. (Reaney s.n. Whiteley, Smith ii.60)
    Richard del Whitlygh 1352 V6 p73

Whitwod
Modern Whitwood. "White, bright wood," from OE *hwīt* + *wudu*. This may be a woodland that was growing thinly and thus showing a bright hill underneath. (Smith ii.124).
    Adam de Whitwod 1352 V6 p14, 68

Willeys
I have not been able to find this place name.
    Henry de Willeys 1275 V1 p126

Wllewro

Modern Wool Row. "Wro" (or "wra") was a remote, isolated place, a nook. Though this would appear at first glance to be "wool nook," then, other spellings of this same name such as "Wlvewro" indicate that the first element is probably from OE *wulf*, "wolf." (Smith ii.249, MED s.v. wrō (n.))

    Margery de Wllewro (f) 1275 V1 p120
    Robert de Wlvewro 1275 V1 p120

Wlvedale

Modern Wooldale. "Wolves' valley," from OE *wulf* + *dæl*. (Smith ii.253)

    Alan de Wlvedale 1274 V1 p97
    Alcok, Alkoc de Wlvedale 1274 V1 p98 may be the same as Alexander de Wlvedale
    Hanne de Wlvedale 1274 V1 p82
    Henry de Wlvedale 1274 V1 p98
    Adam de Wlvedale 1275 V1 p118
    Alexander de Wlvedale 1275 V1 p120 may be the same as Alcok de Wlvedale
    Hugh de Wlvedale 1275 V1 p118
    Lovekoc de Wlvedale 1275 V1 p118
    Mary de Wlvedale (f) 1275 V1 p108
    Reginald de Wlvedale 1275 V1 p148
    Thomas de Wlvedale 1275 V1 p148
    Adam de Wolvedale, Wolfdale 1350 V6 p2, 16
    Alice de Wolfvedale (f) 1351 V6 p59
    Nicholas de Wolfdale 1352 V6 p97
    John de Wolfvedale 1352 V6 p76

Wod, Wode

"One who lives near a wood." *de Bosco* is a Latin form; in the vernacular, his name was likely to be something like *atte Wod* or probably *del Wod* like so many of the other examples here. (Martin 321, Reaney s.n. Wood, MED s.v. wōde (n.(2)))

    Ricardus de Bosco 1274 V1 p97, 142
    John del Wode 1274 V1 p80
    Richard del Wode 1275 V1 p114
    [...] del Wod 1350 V6 p5
    Thomas del Wod 1351 V6 p23
    William del Wod 1351 V6 p38
    Thomas del Wod, Wode 1350 V6 p12, 31
    Isabella del Wode (f) 1351 V6 p26
    Nelle ad Boscum 1274 V1 p91 In the vernacular, this was likely to be *Nelle atte Wode*.

Wodehuses

One who lives at a house in a wood, or possibly works at a building where firewood is stored. There are very many places in West Yorkshire called Woodhouse; this is probably modern Shelley Woodhouse. The plural form seen here is fairly common in medieval citations of the various Woodhouse places. (Reaney s.n. Woodhouse, MED s.v. wōde (n.(2)). Smith ii.250, 218)

    Adam de Wodehusis, Wodehuses 1274, 75 V1 p89, 120

Wodhusum

One who lives at a house in a wood, or possibly works at a building where firewood is stored. There are many places in West Yorkshire called Woodhouse, but this one would have likely developed to a modern form Woodsome, as in modern Woodsome Hall. Plural forms are fairly common in medieval citations of the various Woodhouse places; this one seems to preserve an older form, the OE dative plural

wudu-hūsum. (Reaney s.n. Woodhouse, MED s.v. wōde (n.(2)). Smith ii.250, 218)
    Henry de Wodhusum 1275 V1 p127

Wodthorp
Modern Woodthorpe. "Farmstead near the wood," from OE wudu + ON þorp. (Smith ii.109)
    Henry de Wodthrop 1351 V6 p40, 48

Wolhous
One who works at a wool-house, a place for the storage of wool or production of woolen goods. (MED s.v. wŏl (n.(1)); Reaney s.n. Woolhouse)
    John de Wllehuses 1275 v1 p104
    John del Wolhous, Wollhous 1350 V6 p2, 7

Wolker
Though this seems to be a locative, I am not sure what this place name would be.
    Richard de Wolker 1352 V6 p83

Wollay
Modern Woolley, "glade frequented by wolves." From OE *wulf* + *lēah*. (Smith i.286) But see also Wallay, above.
    John de Wollay "le masron" 1351 V6 p49

Woodheved
Modern Woodhead. "One who lives at the top of a wood." Several "Woodhead" place names still exist in Yorkshire. (Reaney s.n. Woodhead, Smith iii.61)
    Thomas del Woodheved 1350 V6 p12

Wortlay
Modern Wortley. "Clearing used for growing vegetables,"

from OE *wyrt* + *lēah*. (Smith i.298, Reaney s.n. Wortley).
    William de Wortlay 1351 V6 p59

Wrenneclyf
"One who lives near a cliff or slope populated by wrens."
From OE *wrenna* + *clif*. (Reaney s.n. Cliff; MED s.v. wren(ne (n.), clif (n. (1)))
    John de Wrenneclyf 1275 V1 p144

Wroo
Wro (or *wra*) was a remote, isolated place, a nook. From ON *vrá*. (Smith ii.249, MED s.v. wrō (n.), Reaney s.n. Wroe)
    Agnes del Wro (f) 1274 V1 p81
    Adam del Wroo 1350 V6 p2
    Thomas del Wroo 1351 V6 p29
    William del Wroo 1351 V6 p67

Wykes
"One who lived by a dairy farm (a wick)." From OE *wīc*, "dwelling place, abode" which developed the "dairy farm" sense in Middle English. (Reaney s.n. Wich)
    Thomas Wykes 1275 V1 p131

Wyndybank
Modern Windy Bank. "One who lives on the windy hill."
OE *wind*, *-ig* + *banke*. (Reaney s.n. Windebank, Smith iii.88)
    Isabella del Wyndybank (f) 1350 V6 p8
    John del Wyndybank 1350 V6 p9

Wynter
I do not know what place name this is. Nelle is listed with the *de* more than once in the Rolls, so this probably is not a mistake for *le Wynter*. Smith mentions an unattested OE

winter, meaning "vineyard," so this may be a locative name meaning "one who lives or works at the vineyard." (Smith vii.268)

    Nelle de Wynter, de Wynt' 1274 V1 p81 86

Wyrunthorpe
Modern Wrenthorpe. "Wifrun's outlying farmstead," from an OE feminine personal name, *Wīfrūn + ON *þorp*. (Smith ii.157)

    Roger de Wyrunthorpe 1275 V1 p128

Wytewrth
Modern Whitworth in Lancashire. "Hwīta's enclosure" or "white enclosure," from either the OE personal name *Hwīta* or the OE adjective *hwīt* + *worþ*. (Ekwall *Lancashire* 61, Watts s.n. Whitworth)

    Geppe de Wytewrth 1274 V1 p90

Wytfeld
This would be a modern Whitefield, though I do not know which place of that name is intended. The West Yorkshire places of that name are not attested this early. Possibly this is the Lancashire Whitefield listed as Whitefeld in 1292, cited in Ekwall's *Place Names of Lancashire*. "The white field," from OE *hwīt* + *feld*. (Watts s.n. Whitefield, Ekwall *Lancashire* 49)

    Richard de Wytfeld, Witfeld 1274 V1 p91 100

NICKNAME SURNAMES

Aliday
Possibly from an OE name such as *Æþeldæg* (the modern surname from this origin is Allday), or a nickname to one born on a holiday. See also Halyday, below. (Reaney s.nn. Allday, Haliday)
    Ralph Aliday 1275 V1 p132

Ambelour
An ambler was a saddle horse, "an ambling horse," so one with this name could be a stable worker, or someone with an ambling gait. Redmonds discusses this name at some length and adds that it might be a nickname for one who was very easy-going, like an "*amblinge grey mare*," or, ironically, someone who was of the opposite temperament. (Reaney s.n. Ambler, MED s.v. ambler(e), Redmonds N&H 33-4)
    John Ambelour, Aumblour, Aumbelour 1351 V6 p3, 44, 91

Ball
Generally a nickname for one who is round or bald. There is also a locative name *atte Balle* for someone who lives by a knoll. (Reaney s.n. Ball, MED s.v. bal)
    Hugh Ball 1351 V6 p55

Barm
I am unsure about this one. *Barm* was a lap, possibly a nickname for a maker of aprons; it was also a name for a bed, and a word for the froth of fermentation, but I am not finding any surname or nickname uses in MED and OED. I think It is probably a nickname.
    Richard le Barm 1275 V1 p105, 115

Barn'
Possibly "the child." However, the name is abbreviated, so perhaps it is something else. (MED s.v. barn)
    John le Barn' 1274 V1 p81

Baron
Often a nickname for one who is "proud as a baron," but also traditionally given to freemen of London and York. (Reaney s.n. Baron)
    Richard Baron junior   1352 V6 p99
    Thomas Baronn 1352 V6 p73

Bastard
"Not always regarded as a stigma," says Reaney. (s.n. Bastard)
    Alice the bastard, daughter of Margery del Lane (f)
        1351 V6 p34

Bevere
A nickname from the beaver. (Reaney s.n. Beaver)
    John Bevere 1350 V6 p7

Bewe
"Good, fine, fair," from ME, OF *beau*. (MED s.v. beau (adj.))
    William Bewe 1352 V6 p108

Beweshire
"Fair of face," "fair friend," or "fair sir." (Reaney s.n. Belcher, MED s.v. beau (adj.))
    William Beweshire 1350 V6 p3

Blome
This might have been a nickname meaning "a flower or

bloom." However, *blome* was also a word for an ingot of metal. Those who worked with these were sometimes called *blomers* or *blomsmyths*, and this surname is possibly a metonymic nickname based on this occupation. (MED s.vv. blom, blome; Reaney, s.nn. Bloom, Bloomer)

> Petronilla Blome (f) 1275 V1 p121 *Parnell* is the normalized vernacular form given by the translator. The Latin form in the record is *Petronilla*.

Blunt

"One who is blond or fair," from OFr *blund*, blond. (Reaney s.n. Blunt)

> William Blunt 1351 V6 p67

Brese

According to Reaney, this is a nickname from OE *brēosa*, "a gadfly." (Reaney s.n. Breese)

> William Brese 1275 V1 p117

Brid

"Bird," probably a nickname. (Reaney s.n. Bird)

> Richard Brid 1275 V1 p142

Bright

"Bright, beautiful, fair," from OE *beorht*. (Reaney s.n. Bright)

> Henry Bright of Rastrik 1351 V6 p55

Brodfot

"Broad foot," from OE *brād* + *fōt*. (Reaney s.n. Broadfoot.)

> Adam Brodfot 1274 V1 p99

Brok

"Badger," probably, from a ME word descended from OE *broc*; this is not as likely to refer to a "brook" as this seems

not to be a locative, though that name would have been spelled similarly. (Reaney s.n. Brock; MED s.vv. brōk (n.(3), brok (n.(1))).
    Alkoc Brok 1275 V1 p147

Brun
"Brown," from OE *brūn*. A nickname based on appearance. (Reaney s.n. Brown)
    Peter Brun 1274 V1 p87
    Thomas Brune, Brun 1274 V1 p98, 148
    Richard Brun 1275 V1 p117
    Robert Brun 1275 V1 p118
    William Brun 1275 V1 p115
    John Broun 1351 V6 p56
    William Broun 1351 V6 p52

Bukerel
A "he-goat" (buck) with a double diminutive. Possibly a nickname meaning "lecherous, wanton, or lascivious." (Reaney s.n. Buckerell, MED s.v. bukke (n.))
    Thomas Bukerel 1274 V1 p96

Bukke
A male goat or deer; this could denote wildness, wantonness, lasciviousness, or speed. (Reaney s.n. Buck, MED s.v. bukke (n.))
    Ralph Bukke 1275 V1 p143

Bulle
"Bull," from OE *bola*. Perhaps a nickname referring to strength. (Reaney s.n. Bull, MED s.v.bōle (n. (1)))
    Robert Bulle 1275 V1 p112
    Robert Bull 1351 V6 p22

Bulloc
"A bull calf, steer." (Reaney s.n. Bullock, MED s.v. bullok (n.))
    Ralph Bulloc 1275 V1 p124

Burnell
A nickname for one with brown hair or complexion, from ME *brunel*. (Reaney s.n. Burnel)
    Stephen Burnell 1350 V6 p3

Buste
I am unsure what this is, but the MED notes that *bust* or *buste* is "A tax or toll on merchandise sold." Perhaps he was a tax collector or something similar, or someone who spent a lot of time complaining about taxes. (MED s.v. bust(e)
    Thomas Bust, Buste 1275 V1 p126, 144
    John Buste 1275 V1 p153

Champiun
"The champion," commonly a hired representative in "wager of battle." (Reaney s.n. Champion)
    Willelmus le Champiun 1274 V1 p83 88

Child
"Child" in a surname could have one of several meanings, including a young noble, a childish person, or someone known as a young child or minor at his parents' death. (Reaney s.n. Child)
    Richard Child 1351 V6 p52
    William Childe 1352 V6 p97

Chopard
Possibly an Anglo-French nickname meaning something like "clumsy." (Cotgrave s.v. choper, Brachet s.v. achopper)
   Robert Chopard 1352 V6 p97

Cokspur
Reaney suggests this name is a plant name, perhaps for wild clary. (Reaney, s.n. Cockspur)
   Hugh Cokspur 1351 V6 p67

Coldecol
Probably "cold coal," meaning cinders or ashes; possibly a nickname for one who had trouble "keeping the home fires burning"? Or, perhaps, it may be a metaphor for physical coloring. (MED s.v. cōl; e.g. "(1375) To cold coles sche schal be brent"; Redmonds, Yorkshire West Riding p. 152)
   Peter Coldecol 1275 V1 p130

Cort
Possibly a nickname for one who is short, or an occupational name for one who resides or is employed at a manor house or castle. (Reaney s.n. Court; MED s.vv. cŏurt (n.(1), cŏurt (adj.))
   John Cort 1275 V1 p142

Crab
Nickname for one who moves like a crab, or one who is "cross-grained, fractious, ill-tempered" — in other words, crabby. Alternatively, this may mean "crab apple." (Reaney s.n. Crabb, MED s.vv. crab(be) (n.(1)), crab(be) (n.(2)))
   Robert Crab of Birton 1275 V1 p121

Curly

The earliest citation of this word in the sense of "something that is curled" is 18th century. However, a similar form, *crulle*, is cited in the MED, but the spelling here seems unlikely. Reaney suggests this is variation on Anglo-French curleu, "curlew," a nickname from the bird. (MED s.vv. crul (adj.), curleu (n.); Reaney s.nn. Curlew, Curley)

    William Curly 1275 V1 p119

Dade

A nickname referring to deeds, actions, exploits. (Reaney s.n. Deed, MED s.v. dēde (n.))

    Thomas Dade 1274 V1 p91

Dernelof

A nickname meaning "secret, clandestine, or illicit love," from OE *derne* "secret, hidden" + *lufu* "love." Chaucer used *derne love* to describe the Clerk's interests, and Redmonds suggests it was a nickname for a philanderer. (MED s.v. dērne; Redmonds, *Names and History* 35; Jönsjö 80)

    Thomas Dernelof 1275 V1 p130

Dogdoghter, Dogson

Dog- here could mean "dog"; the phrase *dogges son*, or, in modern vernacular, "son of a bitch," was common, and these names may be analogous to that. However, there is also a possible OE given name, **Docca*, mentioned by Reaney; if this given name survived in some form it could be referenced here. (Reaney s.n. Doggett, MED dogge)

    Richard Dogson 1351 V6 p40
    Margery Dogdoghter "mayden" (f) 1352 V6 p68

Drabel

Reaney is uncertain about the origin of this name, suggesting it may be from a diminutive of the OE personal name *Drabba*, or from a diminutive of the term *drab* for a "dirty, untidy woman." *Drab*'s earliest citation is the 16th century. There is also *drabble*, a verb meaning "to soil or trail on the ground," which is cited in the OED as early as 1400. (Reaney s.n. Drabble, OED s.v. drabble)

    Thomas Drabel, Drabell, Drable 1350 V6 p2, 15, 16

Drake

Probably from OE *draca*, dragon, used for a standard-bearer (in battle or in pageants and processions) who often bore a banner bearing a dragon. This could also be a nickname meaning "dragon," or possibly referring to the drake, a male duck. (Reaney s.n. Drake; MED s.vv. drāke (n.(1), drāke (n.(2))

    William Drake 1275 V1 p112
    William Drake of 1275 V1 p147
    John Drake, Drak 1350, 52 V6 p8, 68, 69

Dyne

Reaney suggests multiple possible origins for this name, but the most likely in this context seems to be ME *digne*, *deyn(e)* "worthy, honorable." However, it is interesting to note also that *dyne* is a Middle English noun meaning "noise, uproar, merriment." (Reaney s.n. Dain, MED s.v. dine (n. (1)))

    Gilbert le Dyne 1275 V1 p112

Engleys

"One who is English." Reaney gives several possible reasons why such a name might be given: to denote an Englishman living among Strathclyde Welsh, or by the

French to an English emigrant who might keep the name when returning home. It is unclear why someone in Yorkshire would have this name. (Reaney s.n. English)
    William le Engleys 1274 V1 p86

Feldefare
A nickname referring to a type of large thrush, from OE *feldeware*. (Reaney, Fieldfare, MED fēld(e-fāre))
    Ralph Feldefare 1275 v1 p104

Ferthyng
A farthing: a small coin worth one fourth of a penny. Probably a nickname, which could refer to poverty, stinginess, worthlessness, or something less pejorative. (MED s.v. ferthing (n.), Reaney s.n. Farthing)
    William Ferthyng 1274 V1 p83 88

Fisc
A nickname, "fish," from OE *fisc*. This could be a metonymic nickname for a fishmonger or fisherman. (Reaney s.n. fish)
    Alanus Fisc 1275 V1 p105

Flemang
A person of Flemish birth or ancestry. (MED s.v. flēming, Reaney s.n. Fleming)
    William le Flemang 1274 V1 p83
    Alice, Alicia le, la Flemang, Fleming (f) 1274 V1 p88

Fotihose
Probably "foot in hose"; a nickname of some sort. (MED s.v. fōt (n.), hōse (n.))
    Robert Fotihose 1275 V1 p132

Fox
A nickname, meaning "the fox"; possibly meaning one who is crafty, malicious, or dishonest. (Reaney s.n. Fox, MED s.v. fox (n.))
>Hugh Fox 1274 V1 p92
>Richard Fox 1274 V1 p93
>Cecilia Fox (f) 1350 V6 p7
>Richard Fox 1351 V6 p20
>William Fox 1352 V6 p104

Franceys
A Frenchman, from the Anglo-French *Fraunceis* with that meaning. (Reaney s.n. Frances, MED s.v. Fraunceis (adj. as n.))
>William Franceys 1274 V1 p83
>Adam le Franceys, Fraunceys 1275 V1 p108, 122, 144
>John le Franceys, Fraunceys 1275 V1 p108, 144
>Richard Fraunceys 1275 V1 p149
>Henry le Fraunceys of Staynland 1275 V1 p112

Gaunt
Nickname from ME *gaunt, gant* meaning slender, tall, angular, haggard; or possibly this is metonymic for one who sells gloves, a *gaunter*. (Reaney s.n. Gaunt)
>Richard Gaunt 1351 V6 p2, 18

Gaye
One who is merry, carefree, or possibly lascivious. (Reaney s.n. Gay, MED s.v. gai (adj))
>Gilbert Gaye 1274 V1 p91

Gayne
A *gaine* was an arrow or crossbow; a *gaineier* a farmer. Reaney suggests the name is connected with other

surnames such as Dingain, Engeham, and sometimes Ingham, with the origin being OFr *engaigne*: trickery, ingenuity. (Reaney s.n. Gain, MED s.vv. gaine, gaineier)
    John le Gayne 1275 V1 p106

Gerofer
ME *gilofre*, meaning cloves or a clove (the spice), or a clove-scented plant such as the gillyflower or clove pink. Perhaps the name might have metonymic for a grower or seller of gillyflowers, or a sauce maker who made use of cloves for sauce. Reaney also adds that it could refer to someone "who held land by rent of a clove of gilly-flower." The change from *l* to *r* is not uncommon in period citations. (Reaney s.n. Gilliver, MED gilofre)
    Richard Gerofer 1351 V6 p17

Godale
"Good ale"; one who brews or sells good ale—or perhaps one who uses that as a sales pitch? (Reaney s.n. Goodall)
    John Godale 1350 V6 p13, 67

Godchild
Probably "good child," but the possibility exists that it could be "godchild" as well; some early forms indicate this, though It is impossible to tell with this example. (Reaney s.n. Goodchild)
    Richard Godchild 1351 V6 p30

Godeman
This can be either a nickname meaning "good man" or master of a household, or it can be a patronym from a personal name, from OE *Godmann* or OG *God(e)man*. (Reaney s.n. Godman)
    William Godeman, Godman 1350 V6 p1, 12

Godfelagh
"Good fellow." A nickname for a good companion. (Reaney s.n. Goodfellow)
    William Godfelagh 1351 V6 p17

Godsoule
"Good soul," meaning an honest fellow, a good person. (Reaney s.n. Godsal)
    Roger Godsoule 1275 V1 p108

Goye
"Joy"; as a nickname this might mean a joyful person, a person who frequently used the exclamation "Joy!", or perhaps it is a sarcastic nickname for a gloomy person. It is also possibly a name indicating a relation to a woman named Joia, or a man named Joie. The MED cites the "Goye" spelling. (MED s.v. joi(e, Reaney s.n. Joy)
    Gilbert Goye 1275 V1 p131

Grenehod
"Green hood"; one who wears or sells a green hood. ME *grēne* + *hōd*. (MED grēne, hōd; Reaney s.n. Hodd)
    Luvecok Grenehod 1274 V1 p91
    William Grenehod, Grenehode 1274 V1 p91, 131
    Annabel Grenhod (f) 1350 V6 p1
    John Grenhod, Grenhode, Grenehod 1350 V6 p1, 48, 108
    Robert Grenhod 1352 V6 p108

Gylur
"A deceiver, traitor, defrauder." Also sometimes *the* deceiver, the Devil. Either a disparaging nickname, or perhaps a pageant-name. From OF *guilëor*. (MED gīlŏur,

Reaney s.n. Giller)
    Henry le Gylur 1275 V1 p130

Halt'

le Halt would be one who is lame, but the apostrophe here indicates a scribal abbreviation, so this may be a longer name as well. *Halter* is "one who is lame," and a *haltrere* is one who makes halters for horses; either of these could be a possibility. (Reaney s.nn. Halt, Halter; MED s.vv. halt, haltrere)
    Ralph le Halt' 1275 V1 p142

Halyday

"Holy day," a name commonly given to one born on the day of a religious festival. See also Aliday, above. (Reaney s.n. Haliday)
    Henry Halyday 1350 V6 p12

Hare

It is difficult to pick a specific etymology for this one. Reaney says that it could be a nickname for speed or timidity, "the hare"; it could also be a nickname referring to one's hair. Lastly, it could be a locative, referring to one who "dwells on stony ground," from OE *hær*. In the case of Adam le Hayre, the spellings in the MED indicate that this may have been the latter meaning as the former did not generally use the "y." This spelling could also represent an heir, one who inherits. (Reaney s.n. Hare, MED s.vv. hēr(e (n. (2)), hāre, heir (n.))
    Adam le Hayre 1275 V1 p105
    Robert Hare 1352 V6 p90

Hendebody
"Comely, fair" or "courtly, refined." From OE *gehende* "comely, fair" + *bodig* "trunk, stature." (MED s.vv. hēnd(e (adj), bōdī (n.); Jönsjö s.nn. Hendefelagh, Hendman, Hendwyf)
    William Hendebody 1275 V1 p153

Hering
According to Reaney, metonymic nickname for a dealer in herrings. ME *hering* from OE *hǣring*, *hēring*. (Reaney s.n. Herring)
    Ralph Hering 1275 V1 p132

Herl
"The earl," from OE *eorl*. This is a nickname or pageant name. (Reaney s.n. Earl)
    Robert le Herl 1275 V1 p125

Heud
Probably a nickname meaning "the head," from OE *hēafod*. (Reaney s.n. Head, MED s.v. hēd (n. (1)))
    Isolda le Heud (f) 1275 V1 p129

Hod
"Hood," likely a metonymic nickname for a maker or seller of hoods. From OE *hōd*, "hood." (Reaney s.n. Hodd)
    Adam Hod 1274 V1 p92
    Henry Hod 1274 V1 p86
    Richard Hodde 1274 V1 p96

Hog
"Pig, hog" from OE *hogg*, "pig." A nickname, possibly a metonymic name for a swineherd. (Reaney s.n. Hogg)
    Roger Hog 1274 V1 p86 102

Horne
Metonymic nickname for a maker of horn spoons, etc., or a hornblower. (Reaney s.n. Horn)
    Isabel Horne (f) 1351 V6 p20

Kyde
From ME *kid(e)*, "kid." (Reaney s.n. Kid)
    John Kyde 1275 V1 p130

Kyng
A nickname for one with kingly qualities (perhaps sarcastic), or a pageant name denoting one who performed the role of King. From OE *cyning*, *cyng*. (Reaney s.n. King)
    John Kyng 1352 V6 p77

Launce
Reaney states this is a relationship name from OG *Lanzo*. However, some occurrences of the name seem to be nicknames from ME *launce*, meaning a spear. (Reaney s.n. Lance, MED s.v. launce)
    John Launce 1351 V6 p52

Lawedog
Smith notes that Lawdog may be a nickname "given to a man employed by a feudal lord to 'expeditate' dogs that might be used for poaching." (Smith i.xi, OED s.v. law, v.3)
    Hugh Lawedog 1352 V6 p96

Lene
One who is lean or thin. From OE *hlæne* of that meaning. (Reaney s.n. Lean)
    John Lene 1351 V6 p35

Long
"One who is long, tall" from OE *lang, long*. (Reaney s.n. Lang)
    Adam Long 1275 V1 p106

Marmium
Possibly "monkey, brat" from OFr *marmion*. (Reaney s.n. Marmion)
    Hugh Marmium V1 p129

Maruwe
"Companion, partner, friend." From ME *marwe*. (Reaney s.n. Marrow, MED s.n. marwe (n.(2)))
    Henry Maruwe 1275 V1 p128

Mauduyt
From OFr *mal-duit*, Latin *male doctus*, "badly educated." (Reaney s.n. Mauduit)
    John Mauduyt 1351 V6 p26

Migge
Perhaps this is a nickname for a "gnat, midge" from OE *mycg*, ME *migge*. The nickname might then mean a small or irritating person. (MED s.v. miğğe)
    Adam Migge 1274 V1 p94
    Adam Migge 1352 V6 p79

Modysaull
"Brave, proud, angry, sorrowful or arrogant (the word *mōdi* could have all of these meanings and more) soul," from OE *mōdig* "proud" + *sāwol* "soul." (Reaney s.n. Mothersole, MED s.v. mōdi (adj.), Jönsjö s.n. Modysaul — many of Jönsjö's citations are also from the Wakefield Rolls at various times.)

Richard Modisaule 1274 V1 p87 88
John Modysaull 1351 V6 p67
Peter Modysaull 1351 V6 p67

Monk
Probably a nickname, though in some cases this is occupational. (Reaney s.n. Monk)
Thomas Monk 1351 V6 p35

Morsel
"A bite, mouthful, small piece of food." From Anglo-Norman and OFr *morsel*. (MED s.v. morsel (n.), OED s.v. morsel (n.))
William Morsel 1275 V1 p118

Normaund
"A Norman." From OFr *Normand*, *Normant*. (Reaney s.n. Norman)
Richard le Normaund 1275 V1 p124
John le Normaund, Normand 1275 v1 p102

Utlahe
"Outlaw." From OE *ūtlaga*, "outlaw." (Reaney s.n. Outlaw, MED s.v. ŏutlau(e (n.))
Richard Utlahe 1275 V1 p139

Palmer
A "palmer, a pilgrim to the Holy Land" who carried a palm branch. From OFr *palmer*, *paumer*. (Reaney, s.n. Palmar)
John Palmer 1274 V1 p101

Passemer

A seafarer or sailor; one who "crosses the sea." From OFr *passe mer*, "cross the sea." (Reaney s.n. Passmore, MED s.v. passen (v.))

    Robert Passemer 1352 V6 p108

Peny

A nickname from the penny coin, from OE *pening*, *penig*; ME *penī*. See also Ferthyng, above. (Reaney s.n. Penny, MED s.v. penī (n.))

    Richard Peny 1274 V1 p92
    Henry Peny 1351 V6 p55, 75
    Thomas Peny 1351 V6 p56

Pes

This seems likely to be a nickname meaning "peace.".This was also an interjection, along the lines of "Silence!", so It is possible this is a nickname based on a common saying of Robert's. (MED s.vv. pēs (n.), pēs (interj.); Reaney s.n. Pace)

    Robert Pes 1274 V1 p83

Petit

One who is little. From OFr *petit*, "little." See also Smale, below. (Reaney s.nn. Pettit, Petty)

    John Petit, Pitit 1275 V1 p107, 122, 133

Prest

"Priest," from ME *prēst*, OE *prēost*. Reaney suggests that by this time most examples of this name were nicknames, either for a person with a priestly character or demeanor, or sarcastically for one quite the opposite. (Reaney s.n. Priest, MED s.v. prēst)

Robert Prest 1275 V1 p143
Thomas Prest, Preist 1352 V6 p88, 94

Prigge
Probably a metonymic nickname for a maker ior user of *prikes*: pointed weapons, or pins, nails, and other pointed fasteners. (MED s.v. prik(e (n.), Reaney s.nn Prigg, Pryke)
Adam Prigge 1274 V1 p89

Prudfot
"One who walks with a haughty step." From OE *prūd* "proud"+ *fōt* "foot." (Reaney s.n. Proudfoot)
William Prudfot, Proudfoot 1275 v1 p104, 154
Adam Prudfot, Prudfote 1275 v1 p103, 120

Pudding
A pudding is a kind of sausage, so this could be a metonymic nickname for a butcher, or perhaps for a person who liked to eat puddings. Reaney also suggests a possible origin from the dialectal *puddy*, for a round, fat person. (Reaney s.nn. Pudding, Puddifoot; MED s.v. pŏding (n.))
John Pudding 1275 V1 p150

Pygill
Possibly a nickname from a medicinal herb, European stichwort or great starwort. ME *pigle* from ML *pigla*, *pigula* and OF *pigule*. (MED s.v. pigle (n.))
Henry Pygill 1350 V6 p2

Ragged
One who is ragged; this could mean the wearing of tattered clothing, or one who is physically lacerated. (Reaney s.n. Raggatt, MED s.v. ragged(e (adj.))
Thomas le Ragged, Raggede 1274 V1 p84 88 89

Rathebon
"No satisfactory suggestion can be offered," say Reaney and Wilson about this byname, unenthusiastically mentioning Irish or Welsh origins. The MED includes a *Rob. Rathebayn* s.v. rāthe (adj.); this word bears meanings including "eager, prompt, rash; aroused, provoked; early, soon; important, prominent," and so on. In the case of Rathebayn, however, the second element is probably ON *beinn*, "leg," and so the name would mean "one who has swift legs, a fast runner." But the forms of this name in these Rolls do not seem to indicate descent from *beinn*. Note also in the MED, the word *bŏun*, with meanings including "ready, prepared; eager, willing; ready to go," etc. Could there have been an adjectival *rāthebŏun*, meaning something like "eager and ready"? This certainly does not seem to be an implausible etymology, especially considering the other spellings of this name both in these Wakefield documents and in Reaney/Wilson: *Ratheboun*, *Rathebun*, both of which use attested spellings of *bŏun*. (Reaney s.n. Rathbone; MED s.vv. rāthe (adj.), bŏun (adj.); Jönsjö 149)
    William Rathebon, Ratheboun 1350 V6 p5, 6, 15
    Matilda Rathebon (f) 1351 V6 p43

Reidhod
"Red hood," probably from a characteristic item of clothing. (Reaney s.n. Redhood, MED s.v. rēd (adj.))
    Agnes Reidhod (f) 1350 V6 p4

Robug
"A male roe deer, a roebuck." From ME *rō* + *bukke* (OE rā + bucc). The *-bug* spelling would be unusual, however. (Reaney s.n. Roebuck; MED s.vv bukke (n.), rō-bukke (n.))
    Thomas Robug 1275 V1 p119

Sal
Possibly a nickname meaning "salt," from ME *sāl*. Perhaps a metonymic nickname for a salter? Other possibilities include that this may be a patronymic byname from the pet name Salle. (MED s.v. sāl (n.), Reaney s.n. Sall)
    Richard Sal 1350 V6 p7

Say
Reaney suggests that this is from a place name, Sai. However, this may not be a locative name, as most locatives in these Rolls include *de* or *atte* or a similar mark, though not always (see Henry Sayvill elsewhere in this document). ME *say* or *sai* was a word for "silk" or a type of woolen cloth; it seems possible that this could also be a metonymic nickname for one who sells silk — or perhaps one who often wore it. (MED s.vv. sai (n.(2)), sai(e (n.); Reaney s.n. Say)
    Henry Say 1351 V6 p25

Scab
If this name is Scab (the translator is unsure), that is not unlikely; it was used as a surname, probably for someone with scabby or scaly skin from disease. (MED s.v. scab(be (n.))
    William Scab (?) 1275 V1 p126

Schort
One who is short, from the ME word derived from OE *sceort*. (Reaney s.n. Short)
    Ellen Schort (f) 1275 V1 p129, 140, 146, 155

Schorthose

"Short legging/stocking," probably from a characteristic item of clothing. *Hōse* is derived from OE *hosa, hose, hosu*. (Reaney s.n. Shorthose, MED s.v. hōse)

Henry Schorthose 1275 V1 p105

Schym

A nickname meaning "bright, resplendent." (MED s.v. shīm (adj.))

Hycke Schym 1274 V1 p86

Scutard

Reaney suggests this is a pejorative nickname, from OFr *escoute*, "spy," or possibly from ME *Scot*, "a Scot." The MED suggests it is a derivative of *scut*, "a hare." Either way, It is a nickname. (Reaney s.n. Scotter; MED s.vv. scut (n. (1)), scutard(e (n.))

William Scutard V1 p129

Shakelok

A *shakelok* is a fetter lock, but this name may also mean "shake locks (of hair)." Possibly, then, a nickname for one with nice hair or who was vain. (MED s.vv. shākelok (n.), shāken (v), lok n. (1))

Henry Shakelok 1352 V6 p106

Shepe

"Sheep." A nickname, possibly a metonymic name for a shepherd or a dealer in sheep. (Reaney s.n. Sheep)

Richard Shepe 1350 V6 p2

Slaybrand
This appears to be from an Old Norse word, *slagbrandr*, meaning "a bolt or bar at the door," or "a war engine." (Vries 54, 513)
    Adam Slaybrand 1274 V1 p86 89

Smale
The *de* may be an error for *le*, in which case this is "John the small," a not uncommon byname. However, there are many place names in the area that contain the "small" element, though I cannot find one called simply Smale. (MED s.n. smāl (adj.))
    John de Smale 1351 V6 p55
    Robert Parvus of Crigeliston 1275 V1 p155

Sourmilk
A nickname, possibly for a seller of sour milk, or perhaps with a more figurative meaning. (Reaney s.n. Sourmilk, MED s.v. sŏur (adj.))
    Richard Sourmilk 1351 V6 p56

Spilwod
"Spoil, waste wood." Reaney cites a similar name in Wakefield in 1331: *Richard Spiltimber*. (Reaney s.n. Spillbread, MED s.v. spillen (v.))
    Margaret Spilwod (f) 1350 V6 p4

Spinc
A finch, particularly the chaffinch. (Reaney s.n. Spink, MED s.v. spink(e (n.))
    William Spinc 1275 V1 p139

Sprent

A *sprent* was the spring of a lock, so this is probably a nickname. (MED s.vv. sprent (n.), sprenten (v.))

    Thomas Sprent 1351 V6 p48

Springald

"A siege engine for throwing heavy missiles"; possibly a metonymic nickname for a soldier using such engines. (Reaney s.n. Springall, MED s.v. springald (n.))

    Adam Springald 1275 V1 p129

Stel

"Steel." Reaney suggests this is a nickname for one as hard or reliable as steel. The MED also notes the figurative use of steel to exemplify trustworthiness and endurance. (Reaney s.n. Steel, MED s.v. stēl(e (n.(3)))

    Adam Stel   1274 V1 p80
    John Stel 1275 v1 p104
    William Steell 1351 V6 p35

Stert

"One who lives near a promontory, tongue of land, or hillspur." The various meanings of the word in ME generally refer to projections, knobs, handles, and the like. The MED also includes *stert* as "a derogatory and prob. salacious term for an Englishwoman." Given these meanings, and the lack of *de* or *atte*, this does open the possibility that this is a nickname of some sort rather than a locative name. (Reaney s.n. Start, MED s.v. stert (n. (1)))

    Henry Stert 1275 V1 p131

Stirk

"A bullock or heifer." (Reaney s.n. Stirk, MED s.v. stirk (n.))

William Stirk 1350 V6 p3
Richard Styrke 1275 V1 p129

Strong
"One who is strong." (Reaney s.n. Strong)
John Strong, Stronge 1351 V6 p22, 69

Stut
"Stout" in the sense "valiant, brave." (Reaney s.n. Stout, MED s.v. stōut(e (adj.))
Robert Stut 1351 V6 p60
Margery Stute (f) 1275 V1 p109

Swerd
Metonymic nickname for a sword-maker. (Reaney s.n. Sword, MED s.v. sword (n.))
Richard Swerd 1274 V1 p84

Swyft
A nickname meaning "fast, rapid." (Reaney s.n. Swift, MED s.v. swift(e (adj.))
Thomas Swyft 1352 V6 p2, 92

Syur
"Master, 'sire'"; a nickname, also sometimes used for elderly men. (Reaney s.n. Sire)
Elias le Syur 1275 V1 p128
Geoffrey le Syur 1275 V1 p106, 108
William le Syur 1275 V1 p108

Tagge
A nickname meaning "young sheep," but Reaney suggests a possible personal name which, like the nickname, would also be derived from an OE *tacca* "young sheep." In that

case, this may be a relationship name rather than a nickname. (Reaney s.n. Tagg)
>Bateman Tagge 1275 V1 p155

Talevaz
A nickname from a type of circular shield, possibly for a maker of same. (MED s.v. talevāce (n.))
>Richard Talevaz 1274 V1 p93

Ters
Reaney says this name is from OFr *tiers*, "the third (son)," however one might also note ME *ters*, which meant "the penis," and wonder if this name was at least a double entendre. (Reaney s.n. Terse, MED s.v. ters (n.))
>Nicholas Ters 1352 V6 p89
>Ralph Ters 1275 V1 p127

Thewles
"Ill-mannered." from OE *þēawlēas*. (Reaney s.n. Thewles)
>Thomas Theweles, Thewles 1352 V6 p72, 76

Thrift
A nickname for one of thrift, but the meaning was slightly different than the modern one. It meant wealth, prosperity, good fortune, and luck, among other meanings. (MED s.v. thrift (n.), Reaney s.n. Thrift.)
>John Thrift 1350 V6 p3

Tothe
"Tooth": a nickname for someone with a remarkable tooth or teeth. (Reaney s.n. Tooth)
>Richard Tothe 1351 V6 p40

Trikur
"A tricker": a deceiver or cheat. (Reaney s.n. Tricker)
   Alice le Trikur (f) 1274 V1 p83
   Adam le Trikur 1275 V1 p129

Tyngill
"A very small nail," often called a "tingle-nail." (MED s.v. tingel (n.), Reaney s.n. Tingle.)
   Agnes Tyngill (f) 1350 V6 p7

Uprit
"Straight, not bent (posture)." According to the MED, the meaning "characterized by moral rectitude, firm, steadfast" appears as early as the late fourteenth century, so this may perhaps be what is meant here. (Reaney s.n. Upright, MED s.v. upright (adj.))
   Ralph Uprit 1275 V1 p155

Vigerus
"One who is powerful, strong, hardy." (Reaney s.n. Vigars, MED s.v. vigōrŏus (adj.))
   Peter Vigerus 1275 V1 p122

Waker
"One who is awake, both literally and figuratively; watchful or vigilant." Originally from OE *wacor*. (MED s.v. wāker (adj.), Reaney s.n. Waker)
   John Waker 1351 V6 p55

Waleys
A Welshman. (Reaney s.n. Wallis)
   Philip le Waleys 1274 V1 p80 89
   Stephen le Waleys 1274 V1 p94, 116

Whitbelt
"One who wears a white belt." From OE *hwīt* + *belt*. (Reaney s.n. Whitebelt.)
    John Whitbelt 1352 V6 p82

Whitbird
Possibly "white bird" or "white beard." The ME form of "bird" was more typically *brid*, and *bird* is not attested in ME until the mid-15th century (MED). (It may appear earlier in names; see Reaney s.n. Bird for *Richard Bird*, 1260.) However, the MED suggests that the "bird" form "must be old" and also notes that it appears first in northern manuscripts, so this may be a white bird after all. Alternatively "white beard" is possible, but the spelling is not consistent with this, though forms of this name are very common. Reaney, s.n. Blackbird, lists William Blakebird, 1279, with the meaning "black beard," though this seems as if it could mean "blackbird" as well. From OE *hwīt* + *brid*. (MED s.vv. brid (n.), bērd (n.(1); Jönsjö s.n. Whitberd; Reaney s.nn. Whitbread, Blackbird, Bird)
    William Whitbird 1351 V6 p17

Whithed
"White head," one with pale or white hair, though the *-hed* spelling is unusual at this date and is more typically *-heved*. Jönsjö lists a similar spelling (Wythede) in 1315, and this John is listed as Whitheved in an earlier volume of the Rolls. (Jönsjö s.n. Whiteheved, Jewell 235)
    John Whithed 1352 V6 p85

Wildgote
"Wild goat," from OE *wilde* + *gāt*. This nickname may have referred to lecherous tendencies; the goat was a symbol of fleshly lusts, and of course "wild" often meant

one who was unrestrained, uncontrollable, violent, or lascivious. (MED s.vv. gōt (n.), wīld(e (adj.))
    Robert Wildgote 1352 V6 p82

With-the-hounds⁺
Cum canibus is how the name is written in the 1270s records. By the 1315-17 volume of the Rolls, we see the English versions *With-the-houndes*, *Withehoundes*, *Wytthehoundes*, etc. By the mid fourteenth-century the name has shortened a bit to *Wythoundes* or *Whithoundes*. Out of context these last might seem to be "white hounds," but this seems to be a continuation of the older name that was Latinized as *cum canibus*. In this case the name's original bearer was known for being "with the dogs"; perhaps he was a dog-keeper. (Lister 3, 6, 24, 28, 34, etc.; Jönsjö s.nn. Wythehundes, Wythehogges)
    Johannes cum canibus de Wakefield 1274 V1 p13
    Henry Wythoundes, Whithoundes 1351 V6 p33, 108

Wolf⁺
Lupus is most likely a Latin translation of the English *wolf*. There are many people surnamed Wolf in later (fourteenth century) volumes of the Rolls. This is not typically a complimentary epithet; a wolf was a symbol of rapacity and predation. (MED s.v. wōlf (n.))
    Adam Lupus 1275 V1 p128

Wynter
This could be either a relationship name, as *Wynter* was occasionally used as a personal name; or a nickname, perhaps for one who is like Old Man Winter in some way. (Reaney s.n. Winter; MED s.v. winter (n.))
    John Wynter 1350 V6 p2-3, 4

Wyse
Nickname for one who is prudent, wise, discerning.
(Reaney s.n. Wise, MED s.v. wīs(e (adj.))
    Richard Wyse 1351 V6 p67

Wytlof
A nickname, "white loaf," for a baker of fine white bread.
Compare *Robert Alfwytlof* "half a white loaf," 1296, cited
in Reaney. (MED s.v. whīt (adj.); Reaney s.n. Halfrankish;
Jönsjö 186, 197)
    John Wytlof 1274 V1 p92

Yllewyly
"Malevolent person." A nickname. ON *illr* "ill, bad,
wicked" + ME *willi* "willing." (Jönsjö 198, MED s.v. willī
(adj.))
    William Yllewyly 1274 V1 p92

Yonghare
"Young hare," a nickname referring to speed or perhaps
timidity. OE *geong* + *hara*. (Jönsjö 198, MED s.v. willī
(adj.))
    Robert Yonghare 1351 V6 p24

OCCUPATIONAL NAMES

Bakur
A baker. Gelle's surname is probably a form of Baker, though this is not certain since the reading is unsure. (MED s.v. bākere (n.), Reaney s.n. Baker, Latham s.v. pistatio)
    Robertus pistor de Bretton 1274 V1 p100
    Gelle Bakur (?) 1275 V1 p143

Baly
A form of "Bailiff." (Reaney s.n. Bailey)
    John Baly 1274 V1 p90

Blome
This might have been a nickname meaning "a flower or bloom." However, *blome* was also a word for an ingot of metal. Those who worked with these were sometimes called *blomers* or *blomsmyths*, and this surname may be a metonymic nickname based on this occupation. (MED s.vv. blom, blome; Reaney, s.nn. Bloom, Bloomer)
    Petronilla Blome (f) 1275 V1 p121

Borer
"One who bores or pierces." Probably occupational. (Reaney s.n. Borer)
    Henry Borer 1350 V6 p16

Carpenter[+]
Descriptive byname, written in Latin in the Rolls, but probably *Carpenter* in the vernacular, from ME *carpentēr*. (Reaney s.n. Carpenter, MED s.v. carpentēr (n.), Latham s.v. carpentaria)
    Alcok Carpentarius 1274 V1 p92
    Johannes carpentarius 1274 V1 p89

Magistri Ricardi Carpentarii 1275 V1 p114
Rogerus Carpentarius 1275 V1 p156

Carter⁺
Descriptive byname, written in Latin in the Rolls, but probably *Carter* in the vernacular, from ME *cartēr*. (Reaney s.n. Carter, MED s.v. cartēr (n.), Latham s.v. caretta)

Hugo le Carectarius 1274 V1 p87
Ricardus Carectarius 1274 V1 p86

Chaplain⁺
A priest or clergyman. This seems likely to be a description of his actual work. The name is given in Latin, but the vernacular form is likely to have been *chapelein*, *chapeleyne* or another similar form. In the later records the translator has given us the name in English but it is probably a translation of a Latin form. (Reaney s.n. Chaplain, MED s.v. chapelein (n.), Latham s.v. capella)
Willelmus Capellanus de Halifax 1274 V1 p86 89
Reynerus Capellanus de Kyrkeleyes, de Kyrkeleys 1275 V1 p146, 149
William the chaplain of Laghton 1352 V6 p96
John the chaplain of the parish of Herteshed 1352 V6 p89

Chapman
A merchant or trader. (Reaney s.n. Chapman, MED s.v. chap-man)
Thomas Chapman 1351 V6 p26

Chaumpion

"The champion," commonly a hired representative in "wager of battle." (Reaney s.n. Champion)
    Elias le Chaumpion de Ossete 1275 V1 p145

Chaundler

A maker or seller of candles. (Reaney s.n. Chandler, MED s.v. chaundel-er)
    Robert Chaundler, Chaundeler, Chaunteler 1351 V6 p38, 40, 79

Clerk[+]

Originally this name referred to a cleric. Eventually it came to mean a scholar, secretary, etc. Reaney mentions that it was "particularly common for one who had taken only minor orders" . The modern spelling tends to be Clark or Clarke. (Reaney s.n. Clark, MED s.v. clerk (n.), Latham s.v. clericus)
    Clemens clericus 1274 V1 p90
    Johannes clericus de Cuthewrth 1274 V1 p100
    Michael Clericus 1274 V1 p83
    Michael clericus de Wlveley 1274 V1 p87
    Ricardus Clericus 1274 V1 p83 87
    Willelmus clericus 1274 V1 p84
    Willelmus clericus de Dewesbir(y), de Dewesbyry 1274 V1 p87, 88, 99
    Walterus Clericus 1275 V1 p132
    John Clerk 1350 V6 p5, 67
    Edmund Clerk, the clerk 1351 V6 p17, 58
    Henry Clerk 1351 V6 p44
    Hugh Clerk 1351 V6 p67
    John Clerk de Almonbyre, Clerk de Almonburye 1351 V6 p48, 50
    Thomas Clerk 1351 V6 p38

William Clerk 1351 V6 p40
William Clerk de Walton 1352 V6 p109

Coke
A cook. The earlier examples are in Latin. (Reaney, s.n. Cook, Latham s.v. coquina).
    Thomas Cocus 1275 V1 p126
    Hugo Cocus de Horbyry 1275 V1 p146, 154
    Robertus Cocus de Horbyry 1275 V1 p146, 154
    John Coke 1351 V6 p64

Couhird
A cowherd. Compare *Vacher*, below. (Reaney s.n. Coward)
    Roger Couhird 1350 V6 p16

Couper
A cooper, one who makes or repairs wooden casks. (Reaney s.n. Cooper)
    Elias Couper 1351 V6 p22
    William Couper 1351 V6 p54

Ferer
"A smith, one who works with iron." A ME term from OF *ferreor, ferour*. (Reaney, s.n. Ferrer, MED s.v. ferrōur, -ur (n.))
    Johanna Ferer (f) 1351 V6 p58

Fletcher?
A maker or seller of arrows. None of the sources I have seen use this spelling at this early date (It is typically more like *fleccer* or *flecher*), and I do not have access to the Latin text of this part of the record, so I think this may be a translation from a Latin descriptive term. (MED flecchēr, OED fletcher, Reaney s.n. fletcher.)

Robert Fletcher 1351, 1352 V6 p44, 71
Adam Fletcher of Walton 1350 V6 p10

Forester
An officer in charge of a forest, or one who works in a forest. (Reaney s.n. Forester, Latham s.v. foresta)
Heyne forestarius de Soureby 1274 V1 p90
Johannes Forestarius de Soureby 1274 V1 p92
Michael Forestarius 1274 V1 p97
Phillipus Forestarius 1274 V1 p80
Robertus Forestarius de Sourby 1274 V1 p80
[...] Forestarius 1275 V1 p147
Alkoc forestarius 1275 V1 p126
Hayne Forestarius 1275 V1 p154
Nelle Forestar[ius] 1275 V1 p117
Adam Forestarius de Eppewrth 1275 V1 p120
Alexander Forestarius de Sourby 1275 V1 p140
Johanna Forester (f) 1351 V6 p50
[unnamed] the Forester 1351 V6 p18

Fuller+
An occupational surname for a fuller of cloth, from OE *fullere* and OF *fouleor*. The examples given here, however, are translated from Latin in the original records; this was probably a description rather than a true surname. (MED fullere, Reaney s.n. Fuller, Latham s.v. fullatio)
Rogerus Fullo 1274, 1275 V1 p80, 147
Willelmus Fullo 1274 V1 p83, 105

Gardiner
A gardener, from ONfr **gardinier*, corresponding to OFr (and ModFr) *jardinier*. (Reaney s.n. Gardener)
William le Gardiner 1275 V1 p109, 124

Garderoba

An official of the "wardrobe," a household official in charge of robes and apparel. From ONFr *warderobe*, OFr *garderobe*. (Reaney s.n. Wardrobe)

    Thomas, Thomelyn de, de la Garderoba, Garderobe 1274 V1 p89, 93, 95, 116, 151

Goldsmith

A smith who works with gold or other precious metals. (Reaney s.n. Goldsmith, MED s.v. gōld-smith (n.))

    Robert Goldsmith 1351 V6 p29

Graffard

One who is a " public scribe or scrivener," from ONFr *graffard*. (Reaney s.n. Graffard)

    John Graffard 1275 V1 p108

Grave[+]

Grave was the term used in Yorkshire for the person called a *reeve* elsewhere. In these records the term is always used in its Latin form, *prepositus*, and this is a description of one's office, not a true surname. Eventually, however, *Grave* did become a surname. (MED s.v. greive, Reaney s.n. Grave, Latham s.v. prepositio)

    Adam Prepositus de Neubygg[in], de Neubigging 1274 V1 p83 87
    Adam Prepositus de Rowell' 1274 V1 p84 (Rothwell?)
    Elyas Prepositus de eadem 1274 V1 p93
    Henricus Prepositus 1274 V1 p81
    Henricus quondam Prepositus 1274 V1 p80
    Nelle Prepositus 1274 V1 p80
    Nigellus Prepositus 1274 V1 p90
    Philippus Prepositus 1274 V1 p90
    Ricardus Prepositus 1274 V1 p82, 83, 86, 87, 88, 100

Ricardus Prepositus de Byrkes 1274 V1 p82
Ricardus Prepositus de Scoles 1274, 1275 V1 p82, 120
Robertus Prepositus 1274 V1 p80
Rogerus Prepositus de Ecclishyll 1274 V1 p83
Symon Prepositus de Hyperum 1274 V1 p80 96
Willelmus Prepositus 1274 V1 p80, 100
Willelmus Prepositus de Soureby 1274 V1 p80
Hudde Prepositus 1275 V1 p150
Johannes Prepositus 1275 V1 p107
Matheus prepositus de Sothill 1275 V1 p135, 136
Rogerus prepositus de Heckeshill 1275 V1 p129
Ricardus prepositus de [Ra]strik (?) 1275 V1 p146
Thomam Prepositum suum 1275 v1 p102 ("Thomas
  his Grave" referring to John le Normand)
Walterus Prepositus 1275 V1 p155

Harpour
" One who plays the harp; a minstrel." (MED s.v. harper(e, Reaney s.n. Harper)
  Amabilla le Harper (f) 1274 V1 p83, 85 87, 101
  Robert Harpar 1275 V1 p139
  Ricardus le Harpur 1275 V1 p117
  Adam Harpour, 1351 V6 p25, 40
  Thomas Harpour senior 1351 V6 p42, 109

Hayward
A hayward was a guardian of enclosed haying areas. From OE hege-weard. (Reaney s.n. Hayward).
  William Hayward, Heyward 1351 V6 p48, 52
  Robert Haywarde, Hayward, Heyward 1351 V6 p46,
    59, 99

Henward
Probably a man in charge of the hens. Compare similar names in the MED, including *Henneman, de Henhous, muleward*. (MED s.v. hen (n.(1)), ward (n. (1)).)
    Nicholas Henward 1352 V6 p98

Hewere
"A hewer; a cutter of wood or stone" (Reaney adds, "probably the latter"). Derived from OE *hēawan*, " to hew." (Reaney s.n. Hewer)
    Henry le Hewere 1274 V1 p84

Huswif
"A woman in charge of a household"; this is our modern word "housewife." From ME *hous* + *wīf*. (Reaney s.n. Hussey, MED s.v. hous-wīf (n.))
    Annot Huswif (f) 1351 V6 p23

Jagger
Reaney calls this "a West Riding name." A *jagger* was a "carrier, carter, pedlar, hawker." (Reaney s.n. Jaggar)
    John Jagger 1351 V6 p33

Keeper⁺
A keeper is, according to Reaney, "one employed at a keep or castle." However, the MED adds other meanings that may be relevant here, including "one who holds land as a tenant," one who "has personal responsibility for the care of another," "one who manages household affairs," and so on. The vernacular form is most likely *kepere*. (Reaney s.nn. Keep, Keeper, MED s.v. kēper(e (n.), Latham s.v. custos)
    Dyota custrix (f) 1275 V1 p139

Kittewritt'

A maker of "kits" (tubs, pails, etc.): a "kit-wright." ME *kit(te* + *wright(e*. (Reaney s.n. Kitter, MED s.n. kit(te, wright(e)

    Richard le Kittewritt' of Norlaund 1275 V1 p116

Lister

The Latin text in 1274 includes the Latin form *tinctor*, a translation of the vernacular *Lister* or *Dyer*. Variants of Lister are found in Yorkshire near this time as well as in later Rolls. (MED s.v. litester(e), Reaney s.n. Lister, Latham s.v. tinctio)

    Robertus Tinctor 1274 V1 p87
    John Lyster, Lister 1351 V6 p59, 97

Lorriner+

A lorimer: one who works in small ironware such as spurs or harnesses. From OF *loremier*, *lorenier*. (Reaney s.n. Lorimer, MED s.v. Lorimer, Latham s.v. lorengum)

    Willelmus Lorenarius 1275 V1 p131

Melemakere

A miller, a seller of meal. From OE *melo*, "meal." (Reaney s.n. Meale)

    Adam le Melemakere 1274 V1 p95
    Robert le Melemaker 1275 V1 p105

Mercer

A mercer is a merchant, or specifically, a dealer in textiles. From OFr *mercier*, *merchier* "merchant." (Reaney s.n. Mercer, MED s.v. mercer)

    Philippus le Mercer 1274 V1 p91
    Thomas Mercer 1351 V6 p61

Milner

"A miller." From OE *mylnere* or ME *mylne*, or ON *mylnari*. The name is most common in the northern and eastern counties, which suggests that the latter source is a strong possibility. The earlier records give the Latin *Molendinarius*, but the 1350s form is invariably English *Milner*, which indicates the vernacular form in 1274-75 was probably similar. (Reaney s.n. Milner, Latham s.v. mola)

    Nicholaus Molendinarius 1274 V1 p82
    Rogerus Molendinarius 1274 V1 p91
    Adam Molendinarius 1275 V1 p108, 116
    Gelle Molendinar' (f?) 1275 V1 p155 (Gelle is a female name, cognate with Jillian. The translator says "masculine or feminine?" here.)
    Johannes Molendinarius 1275 V1 p120
    Henricus Molendinarius de Wlvedale 1275 V1 p149
    Gilbert Milner 1350 V6 p5
    Henry Milner 1350 V6 p4
    John Milner 1350 V6 p7
    Richard Milner 1351 V6 p18
    Thomas Mylner 1351 V6 p23
    William Milner, Mylner 1351 V6 p2, 22, 43
    William Milner of Soland 1351 V6 p55
    William Milner of Sourby 1351 V6 p54
    Hugh Milner 1352 V6 p106
    John Milner 1352 V6 p106
    John Milner of Pyksinall 1352 V6 p89
    Gilbert Milner of Stansfeld 1352 V6 p93

Neyler

A maker of nails. (Reaney s.n. Naylar, MED s.v. nailer(e))
    Richard le Neyler 1274 V1 p96

Officer⁺
One occupying an official post, an official of a town, a person of importance. In this case he is the "officer of York." (MED s.v. offīcēr (n.), Latham s.v. officium)
    Willelmus, officiarius Ebor' 1275 V1 p149

Orfeour
Either a goldsmith, or a "maker of orphrey or gold embroidery." From OF *orfevre* "goldsmith," or *orfreis* " orphrey" . (Reaney s.n. Offer, MED s.vv. orfever (n.), orfeverie (n.))
    William Orfeour 1351 V6 p25

Parker
The parker was the park-keeper. Anglo-French *parker* from OFr *parquier*, *parchier*, *parker* "one in charge of a park." (Reaney s.n. Parker)
    Willelmus le Parker de Wakefeud 1274 V1 p90

Paynter
A painter, an artist or decorative craftsperson. From OF *peintour*. (MED s.v. peintŏur, Reaney s.n. Painter)
    John Paynter, Peyntour 1352 V6 p106

Pedder
A peddler, a hawker. From ML *pedārius*, "one who goes on foot." (MED s.v. pedder(e (n.), Reaney s.n. Peddar)
    Dionysia, Dyonisia Pedder (f) 1351 V6 p17, 58
    William Pedder 1351 V6 p17

Ploghman
A plowman. From OE *plōh* + *mann*. (Reaney s.n. Plowman)
    John Ploghman 1350 V6 p2

Pynder

A *pinder* was essentially the animal control officer of the manor, responsible for rounding up stray beasts. From ME *pīnden*, "to enclose, pen," from OE *gepyndan*. (MED s.v. pīnder(e (n.), Reaney s.n. Pindar)

    Margery Pynder (f) 1350 V6 p3
    Agnes Pynder (f) 1351 V6 p48
    John Pynder 1351 V6 p8, 38
    Robert Pynder 1351 V6 p22

Pyper

A piper could be one who plays the pipes, or one who lays them (i.e., a plumber). ME *pīpe* from OE *pīpe*. (MED s.vv. pīper (n.), pīper(e (n.); Reaney s.n. Piper)

    John Pyper 1351 V6 p23
    Roger Pyper, Piper 1350 V6 p4, 42, 72

Queriour

A quarryman. from OF *carrier*, *quarrier*, *querrier* and ML *quarrior*. (Reaney s.n. Quarrier, MED s.v. quarriŏur (n.))

    Richard Queriour 1350 V6 p10

Restar

This seems to have two possible meanings. One, from ME *rēster(e*, is "a person in contemplative life." Another, from *rēstere*, is "One who makes arrests." (MED s.vv. rēster(e (n.(1)), rēstere (n.(2)))

    Henry le Restar, Rest' 1274, 1275 V1 p92, 130

Roller

Probably a maker or seller of parchment rolls. From ME *rolle*, OFR *rolle*, *roolle*, *roulle* "a roll or piece of parchment." (Reaney s.n. Roller)

    John le Rollere, Roller 1274 V1 p90, 102

Rymer
"A rhymer or poet," from ME *rimen* "to rhyme" or Anglo-French *rimour*, *rymour* "a rhymer, poet." (Reaney s.n. Rimer)
    Idonea le Rymer (f) 1352 V6 p108

Salter
"A maker or seller of salt." From OE *sealtere*. (Reaney s.n. Salter, MED s.v. saltēr(e (n.))
    Isabella Salter (f) 1351 V6 p67
    William Salter 1352 V6 p71 (Described in the Rolls as "a common forestaller of salt," so this surname is probably descriptive.)

Schaward
This may be a "forest warden," similar to other compound surnames such as *Wodeward*. *Scha-* from OE *sceaga*, *scaga* " wood," and *-ward* from OE *weard* "guard." (MED s.vv. shau(e (n.), ward (n.(1)), wōde-ward (n.); Reaney s.nn. Shaw, Ward)
    Jordan Schaward 1275 V1 p120

Sewer
"A sewer or tailor." (Reaney s.n. Sewer, MED s.v. seuer(e (n.(2)))
    Matilda Sewer (f) 1351 V6 p46

Shephird
This descriptive byname is written in Latin in the earlier Rolls: "*Uxor Willelmi Bercarii, quia braciavit contra assisam, in misericordia; vjd.*" The vernacular form would have been *le Shephird* or *Shephird*, as seen in the 1350s Rolls. (Reaney s.n. Shepard, MED s.v. shēp-hērd(e (n.), Latham s.v. bercaria)

Willelmus Bercarius 1275 V1 p130
Henry Shephird 1350 V6 p14
William Shephird 1350 V6 p1
Adam Shephird 1351 V6 p29
Richard Shephird 1351 V6 p32
Thomas Shephird 1351 V6 p31

Sklater
" A roofer; one who lays slates." The modern version is usually Slater. (Reaney s.n. Slater, MED s.v. sclāter)
John Sklater 1350 V6 p16, 99
Richard Sklater 1350 V6 p13, 60
Thomas Sklater 1350 V6 p7
Henry Sklater 1351 V6 p55
Elias Sklater 1352 V6 p73

Smith
This name is in Latin in the earlier Rolls. The vernacular would have been a form of Smith, "smith, blacksmith, farrier," as seen in the later Rolls. (Reaney s.n. Smith).
Adam Faber, Adam Faber de Wakefeud 1274 V1 p86, 127
Alanus faber 1274 V1 p90
Willelmus faber 1274 V1 p101
Adam Faber 1275 V1 p130
Ivo Faber 1275 V1 p125
Johannes faber 1275 V1 p109
Ricardus Faber 1275 V1 p129
Adam Faber de Horbiry 1275 V1 p108
Thomas Faber de Miggeley 1275 V1 p152
Johannes Faber de Staynesfeud 1275 V1 p116
John Smith of Thwong 1350 V6 p15
Alice Smith (f) 1351 V6 p20
John Smith 1351 V6 p46, 58

Roger Smith 1351 V6 p56
Thomas Smith, Smith of Halifax 1351 V6 p2, 42, 80
Thomas Smith of Wallay 1352 V6 p109
Peter Smyth, Smith 1352 V6 p99, 102

Souter
A shoemaker, cobbler. The early forms here are Latin. (MED s.v. sŏutēre, Reaney s.n. Soutar, Latham s.v. sutor)
Robertus Sutor 1275 V1 p129
Willelmus Sutor 1275 V1 p124
Walter Souter 1350 V6 p4
Henry Souter 1351 V6 p33
John Souter 1351 V6 p34
Robert Souter, Sutor 1351 V6 p31, 35

Spicer
A spice dealer, an apothecary. (MED s.v. spīcer, Reaney s.n. Spicer)
Juliana Spicer (f) 1351 V6 p58

Stocker[+]
Staurarius is the Latin version; this name means "one who is in charge of the livestock." In English, the name Stocker has other possible meanings; Reaney suggests "one who lives by the stumps" (or, in some cases, by a foot bridge), though the MED also suggests " one who sells stockfish" or, perhaps, a woodworker of some sort. Given the Latin version, we know what was probably intended here. (MED s.vv. stokker (n. (1)), stokker (n. (2)); Reaney s.nn. Stocker, Stock; Latham s.v. staurum)
Ivo Staurarius de Soureby 1274 V1 p100

Tayllour

"The tailor." From Anglo-French *taillour*. Earlier records contain the Latin *cissor*. (Reaney s.n. Taylor, Latham s.v. scissio)

    Philippus Cissor 1274 V1 p84
    Thomas Cissor 1275 V1 p132
    Roger Tayllour, Taillour 1350 V6 p2, 10
    John Taylour 1350 V6 p4
    Adam Tayllour 1351 V6 p67
    Hugh Taillour 1351 V6 p32
    Richard Taylour 1351 V6 p17
    Margery Tayllour (f) 1352 V6 p89
    John Tayllour of Counale 1352 V6 p91

Tanner[+]

In the vernacular, this was likely *le tanner*, "tanner." (Reaney s.n. Tanner, Latham s.v. tannum)

    Willelmus tannator 1274 V1 p84 88

Templer

A Templar, or a servant of a Templar, or one who lives on one of their manors. The Templars, however, were suppressed in 1312. (Reaney s.n. Templar, Templeman; MED s.v. templēr (n.(1))

    William Templer 1352 V6 p108

Toller

A tax, or toll, collector. (MED s.v. toller(e (n. (2)); Reaney s.n. Toller)

    Thomas Tollar, Toller 1350 V6 p2, 22

Turnour

"A turner, one who fashions objects on a lathe" is the most likely origin, however, Reaney suggests that in some cases

this can be "one who turns a spit," or even "one who takes part in a tourney." (Reaney s.n. Turner)
    William Turnour 1351 V6 p46

Tynker
"A tinker." (Reaney s.n. Tinker.)
    Elias le Tynker of Sourby 1275 V1 p114
    William Tynker 1351 V6 p47

Vacher
A cow-herd, from OF *vachier*; see also Couhird, above. (Reaney s.n. Vacher)
    Hugo le Vacher 1275 V1 p130

Walker
A fuller of cloth, from OE *wealcere*. (Reaney s.n. Walker, MED s.v walker(e (n.(2)))
    John Walker 1350 V6 p3
    Roger Walker 1351 V6 p61
    William Walker 1351 V6 p18
    Henry Walker of Waddeswrth 1352 V6 p85
    Matilda Walker (f) 1352 V6 p72

Ward
A guard, guardian, watchman. From OE *weard*. (Reaney s.n. Ward, MED s.v. ward (n. (1))
    Adam le Ward 1275 V1 p117

Wassher
A "washer," one who "washes coins with a corrosive solution to remove some of the precious metal," or a blacksmith's tool. However, the other less pejorative senses of "wash" may be involved here. Note that 3/4 of the people listed in these records with this surname are also

stated to be servants. From OE *wæscan*. (Reaney s.n. Washer, MED s.vv. washen (v.), washer(e (n.))
    Cecilia Wassher (f) 1352 V6 p91
    John Wassher 1351 V6 p25
    Margery Wassher (f) 1352 V6 p91
    Thomas Wassher 1350 V6 p4

Waynwright
A wainwright is a builder of wagons. From OE *wægnwyrhta*. (Reaney s.n. Wainewright)
    Adam Waynwright 1351 V6 p59
    Nabbe Waynwright 1351 V6 p55

Webester
"A weaver," originally female, though by this time the name was used for both sexes. From OE *webbestre*. (Reaney s.n. Webster, MED s.v. webbester(e (n.), Latham s.v. textator)
    Agnes Webester (f) 1351 V6 p48
    John Webester "knave" 1352 V6 p72
    Thomas Tixtor de Hyperum 1275 V1 p112

Wodeward
A forester. ME *wodeward* from OE *wuduweard*. (Reaney s.n. Woodward)
    Richard le Wodeward 1275 V1 p51

Wright
"A carpenter, builder." From OE *wyrhta*. (Reaney s.n. Wright, MED s.v. wright(e (n.(1)))
    William Wright 1350 V6 p14

Wyndelester
Perhaps a windlass maker or seller; the name here has the feminine ending -*ster*, but this did sometimes occur in masculine names; c.f. Webster. (MED s.v. windlas (n.))
Thomas Wyndelester 1275 V1 p113

RELATIONSHIP NAMES

The majority of people referred to in these records by a relationship have names in the following format: *[given name] [son/daughter/wife/relict/man/brother/sister/etc.] of [another name]*, in Latin. An example is *Robertus filius Anot*, or Robert, the son of Anot. These names seem to be simply descriptive, and though I will give some examples of each type ("brother of," "son of," etc.) I will not list every name that follows that basic pattern here.

However, there are other relationship bynames that are closer to true surnames, and I will list those. Examples include "unmarked patro/matronyms" (e.g. Henry Bate) and *–son* names (e.g. Matthew Bateson). Names of this type may have been purely descriptive, or they may have been early hereditary nicknames.

Brother of
Willelmus, frater dicti Thome, petentis 1275 V1 p71

Son of
Henricus filius Ricardi de Northouerum 1274 V1p1

Son-in-law of
Petrus gener Philippi attelidgate 1274 V1 p5

Daughter of
Mariota filia Ade de Almanbiry (f) 1275 V1 p18

Wife of
Matilda uxor Johannis de Horton (f) 1274 V1 p2

Relict of
Avicia relicta Thome de Stanland (f) 1275 V1 p62

Mother of
Alicia mater dicte Emme (f) 1275 V1 p41

Servant of, man of
Hycke garcionem Johannis de Raven[esfeud] 1274 V1 p87
Alanum servientum J. de Rav[enesfeud] 1275 V1 p137
Thomas serviens Thome de Coppele, Thomam garcionem Thome de Coppele 1275 V1 p126, 145
Thomas homo Leticie 1275 V1 p78
Agnes maidservant of Hugh de Langlay (f) 1350 V6 p4

Latin *serviens* may have meant a servant, a tenant holding land by military service, or a sergeant, but *garcio* carries a more menial connotation, that of a boy, a groom, or a servant. *Thomas the servant of Thomas de Coppele* seems to be referred to interchangeably by both terms. (Reaney s.nn. Servant, Garson; Latham s.vv. serviens, garcio)

Heir of
[unnamed] heir of Richard de Northland 1351 V6 p55

Adamson
John Adamson 1350 V6 p15

Agath'
Probably abbreviation of Agatha or Agnes and thus a matronym. (Reaney s.n. Agass)
Hugh Agath' 1274 V1 p87

Aleyn

Personal name from a Welsh and Breton Saint Alan; popular with Bretons who came over with William I, but also very popular in Scotland. (Reaney s.n. Allain)
    Robert Aleyn, Alayn 1274, 5 V1 p87, 126, 132
    John Alayn 1351 V6 p54
    John Alayn of Ossett 1351 V6 p32
    John Aleyn 1351 V6 p61
    Margaret Aleyn (f) 1351 V6 p66
    Robert Alleyn 1351 V6 p18
    Thomas Alleyn 1351 V6 p29

Albyn

From a personal name derived from OFr Albin, Aubin, Latin Albinus meaning "white." (Reaney, s.n. Albin)
    Hugh Albyn 1274 V1 p90
    Robert Albin, Albyn 1274,75 V1 p92, 131

Alcok, -doghter, -son

Pet form for a name beginning with "Al-" such as *Alexander*. (Reaney s.n. Alcock)
    John Alcok 1351 V6 p17, 59
    Nicholas Alcok of Birton 1350 V6 p15
    Isabella Alcokdoghter (f) 1352 V6 p91
    Thomas Alcokson of Ovynden 1351 V6 p23

Aleys

This seems likely to be an unmarked matronymic, "son of Aleys (Alice)."
    Richard Aleys 1275 V1 p148

Amable

Son of Amable. (Reaney s.n. Amabell).
    John Amable (of Dewesbiry) 1274 V1 p91

Amot

I believe that Amot is a nickname for a name such as *Amice*, in the pattern of other names such as *Magot*, etc. But note also that *amote*, *emete*, etc are early spellings for "ant," and *amit*, *amet* are a type of cloak, and so there is some possibility this could be a nickname. See also *Annot*. (Reaney s.nn. Amelot, Amiet; MED s.vv. ampte (n.), amit (n.))

John Amot 1352 V6 p93

Amysson

Henry Amysson 1351 V6 p48

Andrwe

Adam Andrwe 1352 V6 p100

Annot, -knave, -son

Annot is a pet form of *Ann*, which is a pet form of *Annes/Agnes*. Thomas Annotknave is probably Annot's servant, but *knave* can also mean 'son', and there is a Thomas Annotson in the Rolls too. (Reaney s.n. Annatt, MED s.v. knāve (n.(1)))

Robertus Anot 1275 V1 p92, 153, 156 (he is also listed as *Robertus filius Anot*)
Thomas Annotson 1350 V6 p14
Thomas Annotknave 1351 V6 p18

Assolf

Patronymic from the given name *Assolf* or *Essolf*. In a circa 1236 charter, Robert of Knaresborough confirms a stall in the New Market in Pontefract, that is near the "*stallum Assolfi carnificis*," the stall of Assolf the butcher. (Holmes, *Chartulary* 183) The name is often related to Assolf, a minor lord and large land-holder in the area in the 12th century. "Thus, as all the Saxon Kings looked up to Woden as their common progenitor, so did a very large and widespread group of the secondary tenants of Barkston-Ash, Osgoldcross, Staincross, Skyrack, Agbrigg, and Morley, turn their eyes to the now almost forgotten Asolf" (Holmes, "Asolf" 26). In this case, however, we cannot tell if the bearer is a descendant of that Assolf or another, since the name was used as a given name as late as the thirteenth century, and Holmes demonstrates substantial surname change in Assolf's actual descendants.

    William Assolf 1275 V1 p137

Bate, -son
Bate is a pet name for Bartholomew, so this is a patronymic.
    Robert Bate 1275 V1 p114
    Richard Bateson 1350 V6 p2, 42, 44
    Henry Bate 1351 V6 p61
    John Bateson 1351 V6 p22
    Matthew Bateson 1351 V6 p24
    John Batesson 1352 V6 p69

Benet
This is a patronym; Benet is from the name that is, in Latin, *Benedictus* "blessed." (Reaney s.n. Bennet)
    Geoffrey Benet 1351 V6 p17

Benne
Probably a pet name of Benet (Reaney s.n. Benn).
    Richard Benne 1351 V6 p32

Betrisson
Probably "son of Beatrice." (Reaney s.n. Beatrice)
    Adam Betrisson of Walton 1351 V6 p29

Brianman

Brian/Bryan was an OIr name. In this case the name probably indicates the servant of Brian. (Reaney s.n. Brian)
    Henry Brianman, Bryanman 1350 V6 p4, 42

Casson

Probably "son of Cass." (Reaney s.n. Casson)
    William Casson, Casson of Midelton 1352 V6 p82, 84

Clerkson

"Son of the clerk." (Reaney s.n. Clarkson)
    William Clerkson 1350 V6 p2
    Hugh Clerkson 1352 V6 p102

Coleman

Probably from an Old Irish personal name, *Colmán*, adopted by Scandinavians as *Kalman*, and brought to Yorkshire by Norwegians from Ireland. (Reaney s.n. Coleman)
    Jordan Coleman 1275 V1 p112
    Peter Coleman 1275 V1 p127

Cust, -doghter, -son

Cust was a short fom of Custance, or the more Latinized Constance. (Reaney s.n. Cust)
    Isabella Custdoghter (f) 1352 V6 p106
    John Custson 1352 V6 p92

Cusyn

A kinsman or cousin. Originally from OFr "cosin, cusin." (Reaney s.n. Cousen)
    Adam Cusyn 1275 V1 p148

Dobson

Son of *Dobbe*, which is a pet form of *Robert*. (Reaney s.nn. Dobson, Dobb)

Thomas Dobbson de Elwaldhuls 1351 V6 p40
John Dobson 1351 V6 p25
Richard Dobson 1351 V6 p43
Thomas Dobson 1351 V6 p18
Thomas Dobson 1351 V6 p50
William Dobson 1351 V6 p47

Dyconson

Son of *Dicun*, which is a double diminutive of *Richard*. See also Dykson. (Reaney s.n. Dickenson)

John Dyconson 1351 V6 p66
Roger Dyconson of Rastrik 1352 V6 p69
John Dyconson of Staynland 1352 V6 p72

Dykson

Son of *Dick* (*Richard*). (Reaney s.n. Dickson)

Adam Dykson 1352 V6 p80
Henry Dykson 1350 V6 p2
John Dykson 1350 V6 p2
Richard Dykson 1352 V6 p91
William Dykson 1351 V6 p24
John Dykson del Hole 1352 V6 p83
William Dykson del Hole 1352 V6 p108

Dyson, -doghter

Dyson is the son of *Dye*, a pet form of *Dyonisia*. Note that *Dyson* is a "son of" byname and *Margery* is a female given name. This might have been an indication that the name may have become hereditary and no longer merely descriptive. However, in this case we have the other form,

Dysondoghter, to tell the full story: It is a patronym, and she is Dyson's daughter. (Reaney s.n. Dyson)
    Margery Dyson, Dysondoghter (f) 1350, 1352 V6 p7, p 89

Edeson
Son of *Ead* or *Edd*. (Reaney s.n. Edeson)
    Roger Edeson 1352 V6 p104

Elkoc
Son of *Elie* (*Elias* or *Ellis*). (Reaney s.n. Elcock)
    William son of Elkoc de Schakeltonstal 1274 V1 p81 86
    Richard Elcok 1351 V6 p58

Elleson
Son of *Ellis*. (Reaney s.n. Ellison)
    Robert Elleson 1352 V6 p85

Elyot
Elyot (modern Elliott, Eliot) is a diminutive of *Elias*, but may sometimes reflect the OE *Æðelgēat* or *Æðelgȳð*. (Reaney s.n. Eliot)
    Henry Elyot 1351 V6 p32
    John Elyot 1351 V6 p67
    Margaret Elyot (Reaney s.n. Eliot) y 1351 V6 p32

Emma, -doghter, -son
"Daughter of Emma." (Reaney s.n. Emson, Emm)
    Alice Emdoghter (f) 1351 V6 p46
    Isolda Emdoghter (f) 1352 V6 p92
    Robert Emson 1351 V6 p29

Emysdoghter
"Daughter of Emmott." (Reaney s.n. Emmison)
    Matilda Emysdoghter (f) 1351 V6 p29

Faukes
From a personal name derived from the OF *Fauque*, *Fauques* or OG *Falco*, meaning "falcon."
    Robert Faukes 1274 V1 p83, 87, 88

Gamel
Reaney suggests this is from ON *gamall* or ODa, OSw *gamal*, meaning "old." However, this is probably not a nickname, but a patronym; *Gamel* was used as a given name during the thirteenth Century. (Reaney s.n. Gambell; Scott; Harris)
    John Gamel 1350 V6 p2

Gemson
"Son of Gemma." As Alice is female, this cannot be a literal surname; however, there are cases in these records in which women bear their father's patronym as their own unmarked patronym (see Dyson, Dysondoghter), so this could be an example of an inherited name, or just an indication that her father was Gemma's son. (Reaney s.n. Gemson, Gem)
    Alice Gemson (f) 1352 V6 p83

Gepson
"Son of Gepp," a pet form of Geoffrey. (Reaney s.nn. Jeppeson, Gepp)
    John Gepson 1351 V6 p40

Gerard

A patronym. *Gerard* is a personal name of Germanic origin; OG *Gerard, Girard*, OF *Gerart, Girart*; meaning "spear-hard." (Reaney s.n. Gerard)

    John Gerard 1275 V1 p128

Gerbot

The personal name is probably a name of Germanic origin: OG *Gerbodo*, "spear-herald." Gerbot himself is found in the 1274-75 Rolls, sometimes without a byname, but other times with descriptions such as "the Grave of Alvirthorpe" or merely "of Alvirthorpe." Some of his sons bore the byname Gerbot, which seems to have become hereditary, while another had a different name entirely: *John Schirlok*, with a byname which meant "shining blond hair." (V1 p290, Reaney s.n. Garbett)

    William Gerbot 1350 V6 p8

Gibson

"Son of Gibb," a pet form of Gilbert. (Reaney, s.nn. Gibson, Gibb)

    Henry Gibson 1352 V6 p68
    Matthew Gibson 1351 V6 p17
    Thomas Gibson 1350 V6 p7
    Thomas Gybson 1351 V6 p20
    Richard Gybson of Melton 1352 V6 p95

Gilbertdoghter

Daughter of Gilbert.

    Johanna Gilbertdoghter (f) 1352 V6 p96

Gilleson

Son of Gill or Giles. There are several origins; Gille was an Irish-Norwegian personal name found in the North, and also a pet form of Gillian. (Reaney s.nn. Gillson, Giles, Gill)

    Thomas Gilleson 1350 V6 p16

Gillotson
Son of Gill, Giles, or perhaps William. Gillot was a pet form of those names. In this case, though, he appears to be the son of Juliana (see p.18) (Reaney s.n. Gillet)

    William Gillotson 1351 V6 p64

Godeman
This can be either a nickname meaning "good man" or master of a household, or it can be a patronym from a personal name, from OE *Godmann* or OG *God(e)man*. (Reaney s.n. Godman)

    William Godeman, Godman 1350 V6 p1, 12

Godheir
Probably from OE *Gōdhere*, a personal name meaning "good army," in which case this is a patronym. However, it doesn't seem impossible that it could also represent a nickname meaning "good heir"; surnames such as *le Heyr* did exist. Note also the ME word *gōdier*, meaning "a benefactor." (Reaney s.n. Gooder, MED heir, MED gōdier)

    Alan Godheir 1351 V6 p42, 73
    Richard Godheir 1351 V6 p44

Haket
Generally this is an Anglo-Norman diminutive of a Scandinavian name: ON and OSw *Haki*, ODan *Hake*. (Reaney s.n. Hackett)

    John Haket 1350 V6 p7

Hamelin

Hamelin is a diminutive of the OG personal name *Haimo*. This is, then, an unmarked patronym. (Reaney s.n. Hamlin)

 William Hamelin 1275 V1 p124

Hanson

"Son of Hann." The personal name *Hann(e)* was a common name in Yorkshire at this time. The origin of Hann is unclear; it could be a pet name for John or Henry, among other possibilities. (Reaney s.nn. Hancock, Hann, Hanson)

 John Hanson 1350 V6 p16
 Richard Hanson 1350 V6 p3
 William Hanson 1350 V6 p4

Haweson

"Son of Haw." This is a pet-name but it is not clear of which name. Reaney suggests OE *hafoc*, and there are other diminutives of that name that exist. (Reaney s.nn. Haw, Hawson)

 Richard Haweson 1352 V6 p97
 William Haweson 1352 V6 p71
 William Hawson del Burleyghes 1351 V6 p42

Hebson

"Son of Hebb." *Hebb* was a pet-name for *Herbert*. Redmonds tells the Hebson family story on p. 73 of *Names and History: People, Places and Things*; Thomas Hebson probably died from the Black Death, and his daughter Alice was probably the last bearer of the Hebson name. The original Herbert was Herbert de Butterley, also seen in this collection of names. This, then, is a known case of a hereditary surname. (Reaney s.nn Hebson, Hebb; Redmonds N&H p 72-3)

 Thomas Hebson 1350 V6 p15

Henreson
"Henry's son."
>John Henreson of Northland 1351 V6 p42
>Thomas Henrison 1351 V6 p31, 32

Hereward
Unmarked patronymic from OE *Hereweard*, "army-guard." (Reaney s.n. Hereward)
>Nel Hereward 1274 V1 p92
>Robert Hereward 1274 V1 p92, 131
>William Hereward 1275 V1 p131
>Robert Ereward of Wakefield 1275 V1 p125

Hobkynson
"Son of Hobkin." *Hobkin* is a diminutive of *Hob*, a nickname for *Robert*. (Reaney s.n. Hopkinson, Hopkin, Hobb)
>John Hobkynson 1351 V6 p22

Hobson
"Son of Hob." *Hob* is a nickname for *Robert*. (Reaney s.n. Hobson, Hobb)
>Thomas Hobson 1351 V6 p59

Hud, -mayden, -son
Hudde was a common pet-form of the name *Hugh*, though Reaney notes that it may also have been used as a pet-name for Richard. *Hudmayden* likely meant "Servant of Hudde." (Reaney, s.nn. Hudd, Hudson, Introduction p. li)
>Agnes Hudmayden of Longlay (f) 1351 V6 p42
>William Hudson 1351 V6 p58
>Adam Hudson 1352 V6 p73
>Robert Hudson 1352 V6 p73
>John Hudson 1352 V6 p104

Hughdoghter
"Daughter of Hugh." (Reaney, Introduction, xviii; MED s.v. doughter)
 Annabel Hughdoghter (f) 1352 V6 p96

Hughlot
This is a patronymic "double diminutive" of the name *Hugh*, "Hugh + el + ot." Compare *Lancelot*, a similar French double diminutive of the OG name *Lanzo*. (Reaney s.nn. Hewlett, Lancelot)
 Adam Hughlot 1351 V6 p43

Ibbot
Ibbot is a diminutive of *Ibb*, a pet-form of *Isabel*. This, then, is a matronymic byname. (Reaney s.n. Ibbott)
 John Ibbot 1351 V6 p56

Iveson
"Son of Ive." *Ive* is from OFr *Ive*, *Yve(s)*, *Ivon*. (Reaney s.nn. Iveson, Ive)
 Thomas Iveson 1351 V6 p67
 John Iveson of Saltonstall, Ivesson of Saltonstall 1350 V6 p5, 43
 John Iveson, Ivesson 1351 V6 p48, 54

Jakson
Son of *Jack*. (Reaney s.n. Jackson)
 Richard Jakson 1352 V6 p91
 Robert Jakson 1350 V6 p3
 William Jakson 1352 V6 p79

Jonot
A diminutive of one of the forms of *John/Joan*. (Reaney

s.n. John)
    William Jonot 1351 V6 p34

Jon, -doghter, -son
Daughter or son of *John*. (Reaney, s.nn. John, Johnson, Introduction xviii)
    Robert Johnson 1351 V6 p44
    Elena Jondoghter (f) 1352 V6 p68
    Isabella Jondoghter (f) 1350 V6 p7
    Isabella Jondoghter del Skloles (f) 1352 V6 p96
    Richard Jonson 1351 V6 p32
    Robert Jonson 1351 V6 p58
    John Jonson de Lytilwod, Johnson of Lytilwod 1352 V6 p105
    Adam Jonson de Wolfvedale 1352 V6 p105
    Robert Jonson the younger 1352 V6 p92
    William Jonson, Jonson Pynder, Johnson Pynder 1350 V6 p11, 77 A *pinder* was a manorial officer in charge of impounding stray animals. It is unclear whether *Pynder* is William's surname or just a description, but he is sometimes listed as just *William Jonson*. Derived from OE *(ge)pyndan*, "to impound, shut up." (Reaney s.n. Pindar, MED s.v. pīnder(e)

Jordanson
Son of *Jordan*.
    Adam Jordanson 1351 V6 p18

Jud, -doghter, -son
Son or daughter of *Judd*, a nickname for *Jordan*. (Reaney s.nn. Judd, Judson)

Margery Juddoghter (f) 1352 V6 p105
William Judson 1350 V6 p5, 64

Judsondoghter
In this case Margery is not *Jud's* daughter, but instead *Judson's* daughter.
Margery Judsondoghter de Wolfvedale (f) 1350 V6 p12

Kenward
Patronymic from OE *Cēnweard* "bold guardian." (Reaney s.n. Kenward)
Nicholas Kenward 1274 V1 p82

Laweson
Law is a diminutive of *Laurence*, so this is Laurence's son. (Reaney s.nn. Lawson, Law)
Robert Laweson del Dame 1352 V6 p105

Leggard
A patronym from OFr *Legard*, OG *Leudgard*, *Liudgard* "people-protection." (Reaney s.n. Legard)
Hugh Leggard of Bradeforth 1275 V1 p147

Lely
Lely/Lely/Lylie/Lily etc. are probably pet-forms of *Elizabeth*. This then is a matronymic byname.
Richard Lely 1351 V6 p26

Lucas
Lucas was a learned form of *Luke*, so this is an unmarked patronym. (Reaney s.nn Lucas, Luke)
Alexander Lucas 1274 V1 p84 87

Lovekyn

"Little Love" or perhaps "little she-wolf." *Love*, from OE *lufu* "love" was a common female name, and *-kin* a common diminutive. Alternatively, the name might be from Anglo-French *louve*, the feminine of *loup* "wolf." (Reaney s.nn Lovekin, Love)

    John Luvekyn, Lovekyn 1274 V1 p81, 86, 116

Magotson

Magot was a pet form of *Magge* which was a pet form of *Margaret*. (Reaney s.n. Maggot)

    Robert Magotson 1351 V6 p55

Magson

Magge was a pet form of *Margaret*. This, then, is Margaret's son. (Reaney s.n. Maggot)

    Richard Magson de Halyfax 1350 V6 p3
    Richard Magson 1351 V6 p25
    Thomas Magson 1351 V6 p32
    Gilbert Magson 1352 V6 p75

Mahoud

This is an unmarked matronymic byname, from a vernacular form of the name *Matilda*. Some of the many forms included *Mahald*, *Mahalt*, *Maud*, and *Mold*. (Reaney s.n. Maud)

    John Mahoud, Mahaud 1351 V6 p25, 28

Malle

An unmarked matronym meaning "son of Malle," *Malle* being a pet form of *Mary*. (Reaney s.n. Mall)

    Adam Mal 1275 V1 p127 Note that Reaney cites an
        "Adam son of Malle," also in the Wakefield Rolls,

but I do not know if it is the same Adam.
John Malle 1351 V6 p54

Malynson
This is an matronym meaning "son of Malyn," *Malyn* being a pet form of *Mary*. (Reaney s.n. Mallinson)
Henry Malynson de Rastryk 1350 V6 p2
John Malynson glover 1350 V6 p3 Glover appears to be a description of his occupation: he is "John, Mary's son, the glover."
Richard Malynson 1351 V6 p67

Mariot
Mariot was a common pet-form for *Mary*. This, then, is "son of Mary." (Reaney s.n. Marriott)
John Mariot 1350 V6 p16

Mark
Reaney suggests this is a patronym for a son of Mark, but as Mark was a rare name, another possibility is that it is a nickname or a place; the word had meanings including a boundary, a tradesman's mark, a target, a birthmark, and others, many of which could be plausible name sources. (Reaney s.n. Mark, MED s.v. mark(e (n.1))
Thomas Mark 1351 V6 p26

Megson
Son of *Megg*, a pet-form of *Margaret*. (Reaney s.nn. Megson, Meggs)
Adam Megson 1352 V6 p105
John Megson 1352 V6 p68
Robert Megson 1352 V6 p77, 99

Michell

Most likely this is a form of *Michael* (Note the *Michelson* also found in these records), though there is some possibility that this is a nickname meaning "big," from OE *mycel*, ME *michel, mechel, muchel*. (Reaney s.n. Mitchell, MED s.v. muchel (adj.))

    Richard Michel 1351 V6 p59, 91
    John Michell 1351 V6 p46
    Johanna Michell (f) 1352 V6 p105

Michelson

Son of Michael. (Reaney s.n. Mitchelson)
    John Michelson of Routonstall 1350 V6 p5

Miles

Probably from the given name Latinized as *Milo*, but usually *Mile* in the vernacular. However, this can also sometimes be Latin *miles*, "soldier," or from *Miel*, a variant of *Michael*. (Reaney s.n. Miles)
    Thomas Miles 1275 V1 p149

Mocock

This is probably a diminutive for a name which was from OE *Mawa*. Reaney notes *Agnes Mawedoughter* in 1381. *-cock*, of course, is a common diminutive suffix (cf. Alcok, etc.). (Reaney s.n. Maw)
    John Mocock 1352 V6 p105

Moldson

"Son of *Mold*," a variant of *Maud*. (Reaney s.n. Molson)
    Thomas Moldson 1351 V6 p59
    John Moldeson 1352 V6 p100
    Geoffrey Moldson 1352 V6 p105

Moye

I am not sure which given name *Moye* is -- it seems as if it could be a pet-form, perhaps for *Mahew* (*Matthew*)? A *moye* could also be a "stack of grain," but this seems to be pretty clearly a given name of some sort, as it is found in both "son of" and unmarked form. (MED s.n. mŏue (n. (3)))

    Philip Moye 1275 V1 p128, 139, also refered to as "Phillipus filius Moye" on page 108, so this name is seen both as an unmarked patronym and as a Latin descriptive patronym.

Nabdoghter

Nabb is probably a pet-form of *Robert*. This, then, is Robert's daughter. (Reaney s.n. Nabb)

    Alice Nabdoghter (f) 1352 V6 p72

Nelleson

Nalle and *Nelle* are forms of the OIr name *Niáll*, which meant "champion." This name was brought to England via two routes: by the Normans, via Iceland, Norway, and France; and directly to northwest England and Yorkshire by Norwegians from Ireland. The latter is the likely case here, and the common form in Yorkshire is *Nell/Nelle*.

    Robert Nelleson, Nellson 1351, 1352 V6 p42, 71

Nelot

The *-ot* is a common diminutive form. This is Nelle's son. (Reaney s.nn Neal, Nell)

    Robert Nelot 1351 V6 p22

Nicolknave

Nicol was a common vernacular form of the given name *Nicholas*; this would have been Nicol's servant. (Reaney s.n. Nave, Nicholas; MED s.v. knāve (n. (1)))
    William Nicolknave 1351 V6 p59

Norman

From a personal name meaning "North-dweller, Scandinavian, especially Norwegian," from OE *Norðmann*. So this is probably a patronym. (Reaney s.n. Norman)
    William Norman 1275 V1 p116

Odamson

Odam meant "son-in-law." "Son of the son-in-law" seems like an odd name; it makes more sense if Odam is a given name. Perhaps an error for a form of *Oden*, *Odd*, etc.? Yet, it is not completely implausible. (Reaney s.n. Odam, MED s.v. ōthom (n.))
    Nigel Odamson 1352 V6 p72

Otesson

Son of *Ote*, a personal name akin to OG *Odo*, *Otto*. (Reaney s.n. Oade)
    Hugh Otesson 1351 V6 p55

Parkynson

Son of *Perkin*, a diminutive of *Peter*. (Reaney s.nn Parkin, Parkinson)
    Adam Parkynson 1351 V6 p43

Pelle, -son, -doghter

Pelle is a pet form of *Peter*. (Reaney s.n. Pell)
    Elizabeth Pelle (f) 1351 V6 p61
    Thomas Pelle; Pelle, clerk 1351 V6 p48, 109

John Pelleson 1350 V6 p1
Robert Pelleson 1351 V6 p43
Thomas Pelleson 1352 V6 p75
Elizabeth Pelleson, Pelleson doghter, Pellesondoghter
   (f) 1350 V6 p1, 10

Penson
Son of *Penn*, probably a pet name for a *Pernell*. (Reaney s.nn Penn, Penson)
   Adam Penison, Penson 1350 V6 p1

Peresson
Son of *Piers*, a pet form of *Peter*. (Reaney s.n. Pearson)
   Richard Peresson 1351 V6 p20
   Adam Peresson del Crosseligh 1352 V6 p71
   Adam Peresson del Grove 1350 V6 p12

Perkyn, -son
Perkin, a diminutive of *Peter*. This then is a patronym. (Reaney s.nn Parkin)
   Agnes Perkyn (f) 1351 V6 p32
   Adam Perkynson 1352 V6 p87

Peronell
Peronell and *Parnell* are vernacular forms of *Petronilla*, a feminine derivative of Peter. *Pirnel* is possibly another spelling of Parnell. However, note also that *pirnel* is a "central spot in a precious stone," from OF *prunel*, *purnel*, so that example could be a nickname. (Reaney s.n. Parnall; Withycombe s.n. Petronella; MED s.vv. Pernel(e (n.), pirnel (n.))
   Agnes Peronell, Peronel, Parnell (f) 1274 V1 p90
   Elias Pirnel 1275 V1 p126

Prestknave, Prestman
The priest's servant, from ME *prēst* "priest" + *knāve* "servant, attendant." (MED s.vv. prēst , knāve)
    Henry Preistknave, Prestknave 1351 V6 p56, 102
    John Prestknave 1351 V6 p34
    John Prestman, Priestman 1351 V6 p58, 59

Rainer
This is a patronymic byname from the OFr personal name *Rainer*, *Reiner*, or *Renier*, which in turn derives from OG *Raginhari* "counsel, might-army." (Reaney s.n. Rayner)
    John Rainer, Rayner 1350 V6 p11, 13

Reynald
Patronymic byname from a name derived from OFr *Reinald*, *Reynaud*. (Reaney s.n. Reynold)
    John Reynald, Reynard, Raynald 1351 V6 p1, 22, 25, 54

Robin
Robin is a diminutive of *Robert*, so this is a patronymic byname. (Reaney s.n. Robins)
    Richard Robin, Robyn 1351 V6 p29, 55

Robynson
"Son of Robin." (Reaney s.n. Robinson)
    John Robynson 1352 V6 p72

Rogerson
"Son of Roger." (Reaney s.n. Rogerson)
    Thomas Rogerson 1351 V6 p23
    William Rogerson of Langlay 1351 V6 p34
    Matthew Rogerson 1352 V6 p91
    Thomas Rogerson the younger 1352 V6 p80

Sampson

"The name was popular in Yorkshire and the eastern counties where it was introduced by Bretons after the conquest." This is a patronymic byname from OFr *Sanson*, *Samson*, name of a Welsh bishop later venerated as a saint. The name may have originated from the Biblical figure, or may be of Celtic origin. (Reaney s.n. Sampson)

    Thomas Sampson 1274 V1 p84

    William Samson de Grenewod 1350 V6 p4

Sarasson

Probably "son of Sara." Probably not "Saracen." (Reaney s.nn. Sarson, Sara)

    Robert Sarasson 1351 V6 p17

Sare

"Sara," so this is an unmarked matronym. (Reaney s.n. Sara)

    Thomas Sare V1 p129

Syeger

Perhaps this is the name, modern Siggers or Siger, that Reaney relates to several possible personal names: OE *Sigegār*, ON *Sigarr*, and others. (Reaney s.n. Siggers)

    Adam Syeger of Grigelston V1 p129

Symson

"Son of *Simm*," a nickname for *Simon*. (Reaney s.n. Simpson)

    John Symson 1351, 52 V6 p22, 69

Tissotson

This seems to be a patronymic, but I cannot find the name Tissot. Could it be a matronym, a pet form of a name such as *Lettice*?

    John Tissotson 1352 V6 p91

Tomasson, Tomson

"Son of *Thomas* or *Tom*." (Reaney s.n. Thomason, Thompson)

    Richard Thomasson of Sandale 1352 V6 p85
    John Tomasson, Tomson, Tommasson, Thomasson
        1351 V6 p42, 62, 66, 83, 87 (invariably as
        "Tomasson clerk," "Thomasson clerk," etc.)
    John Tomasson 1352 V6 p108
    Matthew Tomasson 1352 V6 p105
    John Tomasson of Saltonstall 1352 V6 p108
    John Tomson 1350 V6 p4
    William Tomson 1350 V6 p5, 9
    William Tomson of Grenwod 1350 V6 p5
    Henry Tomson 1352 V6 p90

Tomelynson

"Son of *Tomlin*" (a double diminutive of *Tom*, which is itself a diminutive of *Thomas*). (Reaney s.nn. Tomlinson, Tomlin)

    Matthew Tomelynson 1350 V6 p2

Tonson

Perhaps an error for Tomson?

    John Tonson 1350 V6 p1

Torald
Unmarked patronym. The name descends from the ON personal name *Þóraldr* or *Þorváldr*, "Thor-ruler." (Reaney s.n. Thorold)
    Philip Torald 1275 V1 p132
    Thomas Torald 1352 V6 p100

Urebrother
"Our brother," typically meaning a person related by blood or marriage, (MED s.v. ōur(e (pron.))
    Henry Urebrother, Hourebrother 1274 V1 p96, 107

Wade
Unmarked patronym, from a name originally from OE *Wada* or OG *Wado*. A *wade* is also a ford, but this name is not marked as a locative. (Reaney s.n. Wade)
    Adam Wade 1351 V6 p20
    Hugh Wade 1350 V6 p5
    Nicholas Wade 1350 V6 p2
    Thomas Wade 1352 V6 p72
    William Wade 1351 V6 p20

Walding
An unmarked patronym. The name is from a name descended from OE *Wealding*, or possibly confused with one from OG *Waldin*. (Reaney s.n. Walding)
    Gilbert Walding 1275 V1 p126

Walhot
Probably an unmarked patronym; Reaney suggests it may be an *-et* diminutive of the Anglo-Scandinavian name *Walþēof*. (Reaney s.n. Wallet)
    John Walhot 1275 V1 p109, 126

Walter

An unmarked patronymic, from a common name post-Conquest. (Reaney s.n. Walter)
    Agnes Walter (f) 1351 V6 p23

Warynson

Warin was an Anglo-French name from a common Norman name. (Reaney s.n. Wareing)
    John Warynson 1352 V6 p76

Watson

"Son of *Wat*," a diminutive of *Walter*. (Reaney s.n. Watson)
    John Watson 1352 V6 p99
    John Watson of Wakefeld 1350 V6 p10

Wilkson

Wilk may be a short form of the rare name *Willoc*, or perhaps a given name in its own right (Reaney cites *Wylke de Chyrchele*, 1246). (Reaney s.n. Wilk)
    John Wilkson of Collerslay 1351 V6 p33

Wilkynson

Wilkin is a diminutive of *William* or *Will*. (Reaney s.nn. Wilkin, Wilkinson)
    John Wilkynson 1352 V6 p82

Willeson

Will is, of course, a short form of *William*. (Reaney s.n. Wilson)
    John Willeson 1350 V6 p3
    Thomas Willeson 1351 V6 p46, p58
    William Willeson 1351 V6 p38

Thomas Willeson de Alstonlay 1351 V6 p65
John Willeson del Hole 1351 V6 p60

Williamson
Richard William's son 1351 V6 p64 (The apostrophe is probably a 20th century editorial addition.)
Thomas Williamson 1351 V6 p28

Wlf
Either a nickname meaning "wolf," or a patronymic from the ON personal name *Úlfr*. Reaney suggests that the nickname is more likely to be in the form "le wolf," and the Norse name would have been likely to be found in Yorkshire, so I think this is probably a patronymic. (Reaney s.nn. Wolf, Ulph; Bardsley Dictionary s.n. Wolff; MED s.v. wŏlf (n.))
Roger Wlf 1275 V1 p105
William Wolf, Wolfe 1351 V6 p17, 46

Wolmer
Probably from the OE personal name *Wulfmǣr*. (Reaney s.n. Woolmer)
Thomas Wolmer 1351 V6 p55

Wylcokson
Son of *Wilcock*, which was a pet name for *William*. (Reaney s.nn. Wilcockson, Wilcock)
John Wylcokson of Ourom 1352 V6 p89

Wylimot
Son of *Wylimot*, a pet name for *Willelm* or *William*. (Reaney s.n. Willmot)
Robert Wylimot, Wylymot 1351 V6 p30, 66

Wymes
Note Wymeswold, in Leicestershire, which is from the OE personal name *Wīgmund*, in the genitive form, + OE *wald*. If the OE name survived into the ME period, this is probably a patronymic name. Another possibility, less likely, is that it is related to Wemyss, from the lands of Wemyss in fife. (Reaney s.n. Wemyss, Watts s.n. Wymeswold)
    Adam Wymes of Staynford 1275 V1 p127

DOUBLE PATRONYMS

Double patronyms, in the form "*X*son *X*son" (or *X*son followed by an unmarked patronym) are seen in the 1350-52 Rolls, but not in the thirteenth century rolls (Reaney xxi).These names essentially give a two-generation patronym instead of the more common single generation. For example, says Reaney, "the sons of William Jonson are named William Willeson Johanson and Benedict Willeson Johnson" (li); in other words, William, John's son, fathered William and Benedict, sons of Will, who was son of John. I will list each of these type of names separately.

Thomas Jonson Dobson
"Son of *John* who was the son of *Dobbe*." Dobbe was a pet name for *Robert* and was fairly common in Yorkshire. (Reaney s.nn. Johnson, Dobb, Dobson) 1351 V6 p43

Adam Jonson Dykson
"Son of *John* who was the son of *Dyk*." Dyk was a pet name for *Richard*. (Reaney s.nn. Johnson, Dick, Dickson) 1352 V6 p90

William Hughson Elye
"Son of *Hugh*, son of *Ely* (Elijah)." (Reaney s.nn. Ely, Hughson) 1352 V6 p85

John Judson Elyot
"Son of *Judd* who was the son of *Elyot*." Jud was a pet name for *Jordan*, and Elyot was a pet name for *Elias*. (Reaney s.nn. Judd, Judson, Eliot) 1350 V6 p3

Robert Jonson Emmot
"Son of *John* who was the son of *Emmot*." Emmot was a pet name for *Emma*. (Reaney s.nn. Johnson, Emmatt) 1352 V6 p109

Matthew Thomasson Gibson
Double patronymic, meaning "son of Thomas who was the son of Gibb." (Reaney s.nn. Thomason, Gibson) 1352 V6 p105

John Johnson Hudson of Horbure, Jonson Hudson
"Son of *John* who was the son of *Hudde*." Hudde was a pet name for *Hugh* and was fairly common. (Reaney s.nn. Johnson, Hanson, Hudd, Hudson) 1351 V6 p30, 32

William Jonson Pelleson
"Son of *John* who was the son of *Pell*." Pell was a pet name for *Peter*. (Reaney s.nn. Johnson, Pellson) 1351 V6 p18

Elias Symson Judson
"Elias son of *Simm* son of *Judd*." Simm was a pet name for *Simon*. Judd or *Jutt* was a nickname for *Jordan*. (Reaney s.nn. Simpson, Judson, Judd) 1350 V6 p14

John Dikson Pereson
"Son of *Dick* son of *Piers*." Piers is a short from of *Peter*. 1352 V6 p92

Henry Tomasson Roboson
"Son of *Thomas* who was the son of *Robert* or *Robe*." Robe was a pet form of Robert. (Reaney s.nn. Thomason, Robson, Robinson, Robeson) 1352 V6 p92

Henry Adamson Wade
"Son of *Adam* who was the son of *Wade*." Wade was probably derived from the Old English given name *Wada*. (Reaney s.n. Wade) 1352 V6 p105

John Adamson Willeson
"Son of *Adam* who was the son of *Will*." 1352 V6 p90

William Hanson Hudson
"Son of *Hann* who was the son of *Hudde*." The personal name *Hann(e)* was a common name in Yorkshire at this time. The origin of *Hann* is debatable; it could be a pet name for John or Henry, among other possibilities. *Hudde* was a pet name for *Hugh* and was fairly common. (Reaney s.nn. Hancock, Hann, Hanson, Hudd, Hudson) 1351 V6 p46

Appendix I: Bibliography

Baildon, William Paley, ed. and trans. *Court Rolls of The Manor of Wakefield, Volume I, 1274-1297*. Leeds: Yorkshire Archæological Society, 1901. Print.

Bardsley, Charles Wareing. *A Dictionary of English and Welsh Surnames: With Special American Instances*. London: Oxford UP, 1901. *Google Books*. Web. 15 March 2009.

Brachet, A. *An Etymological Dictionary of the French Language*. Oxford, 1882. *Google Books*. Web. 15 April 2008.

Cotgrave, Randle. *A Dictionarie of the French and English Tongues*. London, 1611. *SCA Renaissance Dance Homepage*. Ed. Greg Lindahl. Web. 15 April 2008.

Crowther, George H. *A Descriptive History of the Wakefield Battles; and a Short Account of This Ancient and Important Town*. Wakefield, 1886. Transcribed by Beryl Thompson. Web. 8 July 2008. <http://members.pcug.org.au/~pfthomps/wakefield/wakefd.pdf>.

Denholm-Young, Noel. *Seignorial Administration in England*. 1937. London: Cass, 1963. Print.

Ekwall, Eilert. *Concise Oxford Dictionary of English Place Names*. 4th ed. Oxford: Oxford UP, 1960. Print.

---. *The Place-Names of Lancashire*. Manchester: UP, 1922. Print.

Gies, Frances, and Joseph Gies. *Marriage and Family in the Middle Ages*. New York: Harper, 1987. Print.

Goldberg, P.J.P. *Women, Work, and Life Cycle in a Medieval Economy: Women in York and Yorkshire c. 1300-1520*. 1992. Oxford: Oxford UP, 2002. Print.

Habberjam, Moira, Mary O'Regan, and Brian Fraser, eds. *Court Rolls of the Manor of Wakefield: From October 1350 to September 1352*. Leeds: Yorkshire Archaeological Soc., 1987. Print.

Harris, Karen. "Bynames found in the 1296 Lay Subsidy Rolls for Rutland, England (patronyms)." Society for Creative Anachronism. Web. 1 May 2008.

Hey, David. *Family Names and Family History*. London: Hambledon, 2000. Print.

"History of St. Oswald and St. Oswald's Church, Sowerby." *St. Oswald's Church, Sowerby*. Parochial Church Council of St. Oswald's Church, Sowerby. Web. 8 April 2008.

Hjertstedt, Ingrid. *Middle English Nicknames in the Lay Subsidy Rolls for Warwickshire*. Acta Universitatis Upsaliensis, 63. Uppsala: Academiae Ubsaliensis, 1987. Print.

Holmes, Richard. "Asolf or Essolf, a Yorkshire Minor Lord of the Twelfth Century." *The Publications of the Thoresby Society, Volume IX: Miscellanea*. Leeds, 1899. 23. *Google Books*. Web. 15 April 2008.

---, ed. *The Chartulary of St. John of Pontefract*. Leeds, 1899. *Google Books*. Web. 15 April 2008.

Jewell, Helen M., ed. *Court Rolls of the Manor of Wakefield: From September 1348 to September 1350*. Leeds: Yorkshire Archaeological Soc., 1981. Print.

Jönsjö, Jan. *Studies on Middle English Nicknames I. Compounds*. Lund studies in English, 55. Lund: Gleerup, 1979. Print.

Latham, R.E. *Revised Medieval Latin Word-List from British and Irish Sources*. London: Oxford UP, 1980. Print.

Lister, John, ed. and trans. *Court Rolls of The Manor of Wakefield, Volume IV, 1315-1317*. Leeds: Yorkshire Archæological Soc., 1930. Print.

Martin, Charles Trice. "Latin Forms of English Surnames." *The Record Interpreter: A Collection of Abbreviations, Latin Words and Names Used in*

English Historical Manuscripts and Records. London, 1892. *Google Books.* Web. 18 March 2009.

The Middle English Dictionary. The Middle English Compendium. University of Michigan, 2001. Web.

Mills, A.D. *A Dictionary of British Place Names.* Oxford: Oxford UP, 2003. Print.

OED Online. Oxford: Oxford UP. Web.

Reaney, P.H. *A Dictionary of English Surnames.* 3rd Edition Rev. by R.M. Wilson. Oxford: Oxford UP, 1997. Print.

---. *The Origin of English Surnames.* London: Routledge, 1967. Print.

Redmonds, George. *English Surnames Series I: Yorkshire West Riding.* London: Phillimore, 1973. Print.

---. *Names and History: People, Places and Things.* London: Hambledon, 2004. Print.

Scott, Brian. "Men's Given Names from early 13th Century England." Society for Creative Anachronism. Web. 1 May 2008.

Smith, A. H. *English Place-Name Elements, Part I: Á-Iw.* English Place-Name Society, v. 25. Cambridge: Cambridge UP, 1956. Print.

---. *English Place-Name Elements, Part II: Jafn-Ytri.* English Place-Name Society, v. 26. Cambridge: Cambridge UP, 1956. Print.

---. *The Place-Names of the East Riding of Yorkshire and York*. English Place-Name Society, v. 14. Cambridge: Cambridge UP, 1937. Print.

---. *The Place-Names of the West Riding of Yorkshire, Part I: Lower and Upper Strafforth and Staincross Wapentakes*. English Place-Name Society, v. 30. Cambridge: Cambridge UP, 1961. Print.

---. *The Place-Names of the West Riding of Yorkshire, Part II: Osgoldcross and Agbrigg Wapentakes*. English Place-Name Society, v. 31. Cambridge: Cambridge UP, 1961. Print.

---. *The Place-Names of the West Riding of Yorkshire, Part III: Morley Wapentake*. English Place-Name Society, v. 32. Cambridge: Cambridge UP, 1961. Print.

---. *The Place-Names of the West Riding of Yorkshire, Part IV: Barkston-Ash, Skyrack and Ainsty Wapentakes*. English Place-Name Society, v. 33. Cambridge: Cambridge UP, 1961. Print.

---. *The Place-Names of the West Riding of Yorkshire, Part V: Upper and Lower Claro Wapentakes*. English Place-Name Society, v. 34. Cambridge: Cambridge UP, 1961. Print.

---. *The Place-Names of the West Riding of Yorkshire, Part VI: East and West Staincliffe and Ewcross*

Wapentakes. English Place-Name Society, v. 35. Cambridge: Cambridge UP, 1961. Print.

---. *The Place-Names of the West Riding of Yorkshire, Part VII, Introduction, Bibliography, Etc.* English Place-Name Society, v. 36. Cambridge: Cambridge UP, 1962. Print.

---. *The Place-Names of the West Riding of Yorkshire. Incorporating the East and North Ridings. Part 8, Index of West Riding Place-Names*. English Place-Name Society, v. 37. Cambridge: Cambridge UP, 1963. Print.

Vries, Jan de. *Altnordisches etymologisches Wörterbuch*. Leiden: Brill, 1962. 54, 513. *Google Books*. Web. 30 July 2007.

Wakefield Court Roll Section of the Yorkshire Archaeological Society. Yorkshire Archaeological Society, n.d. Web. 16 April 2010.

Walker, Sue Sheridan, ed. *Court Rolls of the Manor of Wakefield: From October 1331 to September 1333*. Leeds: Yorkshire Archaeological Soc., 1982. Print.

Watts, V. E., John Insley, and Margaret Gelling. *The Cambridge Dictionary of English Place-Names Based on the Collections of the English Place-Name Society*. Cambridge: Cambridge UP, 2004. Print.

Weekley, Ernest. *Surnames*. New York: Dutton, 1937. Print.

Withycombe, E.G. *The Oxford Dictionary of English Christian Names*. 3rd Ed. Oxford: Oxford UP, 1977. Print.

Appendix II: Maps

Map 1. The location of historic Yorkshire and the three Ridings in relation to the rest of England.

Map 2. The location of Wakefield Manor within the West Riding.

www.ingramcontent.com/pod-product-compliance
Lightning Source LLC
Chambersburg PA
CBHW020743100426
42735CB00037B/328